GRUBER'S
SAT *
2nd Edition

WORD MASTER

The Most Effective Way to Learn the Most Important SAT Vocabulary Words

*SAT is a registered trademark of the College Entrance Examination Board. The College Entrance Examination Board is not associated with and does not endorse this book.

GARY R. GRUBER, PHD

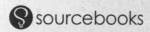
sourcebooks

Published by Sourcebooks, Inc.
P.O. Box 4410, Naperville, Illinois 60567-4410
(630) 961-3900
Fax: (630) 961-2168
www.sourcebooks.com

The Library of Congress has catalogued the first edition as follows:

Gruber, Gary R.
  Gruber's SAT word master : the most effective way to learn the most important sat vocabulary words / by Gary R. Gruber.
     p. cm.
  1. SAT (Educational test)—Study guides. 2. English language—Examinations—Study guides. 3. Vocabulary tests—Study guides. I. Title. II. Title: SAT word master.
  LB2353.57.G786 2008
  378.1'662—dc22

                              2009015899

Printed and bound in the United States of America.
VP 10 9 8 7 6 5 4 3 2 1

Recent and Forthcoming Study Aids From Dr. Gary Gruber

Gruber's Essential Guide to Test Taking: Grades 3–5

Gruber's Essential Guide to Test Taking: Grades 6–9

Gruber's Complete SAT Guide 2011 (14th Edition)

Gruber's Complete ACT Guide 2011 (2nd Edition)

Gruber's SAT 2400 (2nd Edition)

Gruber's Complete SAT Critical Reading Workbook (2nd Edition)

Gruber's Complete SAT Math Workbook (2nd Edition)

Gruber's Complete SAT Writing Workbook (2nd Edition)

Gruber's Complete SAT Guide 2012 (15th Edition)

Gruber's Complete ACT Guide 2012 (3rd Edition)

Gruber's Complete GRE Guide 2012

www.sourcebooks.com

www.drgarygruber.com

www.mymaxscore.com

Contents

Introduction

This book is aimed at tremendously increasing your vocabulary and helping you develop a fast way to figure out the meanings of words if you don't know them.

The Gruber Prefixes, Roots, and Suffixes can give you the meaning of more than 200,000 words! Vocabulary strategies will allow you to figure out meanings of words you don't know. And if you prefer to strictly memorize words, there's a list of 2300 words that appear on the SAT and other standardized tests.

Here's an example of a word strategy: Suppose you don't know the meaning of the word "inextricable." How would you figure it out? Well, maybe you'd say that "in" is a prefix that means "not." But what about "extric"? You'd associate that word with another word: "extra." But "not" to "extra" does not make sense. So you don't give up—you try another word for "extric," such as "extract." "Not" to "extract" does make sense—it means "inseparable," or unable to take apart!

Here's an example of a way to use one of the Gruber Prefixes and Roots: Suppose you want to find the meaning of the word "precursory." The prefix and root in this word are part of the prefixes and roots list that gives you the meaning of over 200,000 words:

"Pre" means "before"
"Curs" means "to run"

So "precursory" means running before or going before.

If you read through this book chapter by chapter, you will increase your vocabulary tremendously.

Purpose of This Book

The purpose of this book is to markedly increase your vocabulary and provide a way for you to figure out the meanings of words you don't know through various powerful word strategies. It is very important to have a good vocabulary when taking the SAT. In this book, you will find that you don't necessarily have to know the meanings of many words: you can figure them out in the context of the rest of the sentence or passage. You may also figure out the meanings of words or how to use them in a sentence through the strategies that are in this book.

Dr. Gruber has developed powerful, time-tested strategies for vocabulary building, including his 200,000 word vocabulary builder through prefix-root development. He is the originator of the critical thinking skills used on standardized tests and the leading authority on test preparation.

Note that this book can be used effectively for learning shortcuts and strategies and practice for all vocabulary-based questions on any test, or it can be used to build your vocabulary for your own purposes.

What This Book Contains

How to Use This Book Most Effectively

1. Read through the Introduction.

2. Learn as many of the fifty prefixes, roots, and suffixes as you can.

3. Take the Prefix-Root-Suffix Test and see how you do.

4. Learn the Hot Prefixes and Roots.

5. By all means, learn the three Vocabulary Strategies.

6. Try to answer the questions in the Practice Test with the Gruber Prefixes and Roots.

7. Try to learn some of the words in the Word List. Try to memorize words that have the same meaning.

8. If you have time, try to learn some of the words in the 2300 Word List—see if you can figure out some of these words through what you learned in the previous sections.

9. Take some of the Vocabulary Tests.

10. Read through A List of Words Appearing More Than Once on the SAT.

11. Look at the Words Commonly Confused.

VOCABULARY BUILDING THAT IS GUARANTEED TO RAISE YOUR SAT SCORE

Knowing Word Meanings Is Essential for a Higher SAT Score

Improving your vocabulary is essential if you want to get a high score on the Critical Reading Section of the SAT. We shall explain why this is so.

The Critical Reading Section part of the SAT consists of two different question types: Sentence Completions and Reading Comprehension. Almost all SAT exam takers come across many "tough" words in this part, whose meanings they do not know. These students lose many points because if they do not know the meanings of the words in the questions, they aren't able to answer the questions confidently—and they are likely to answer incorrectly.

Every correct answer on the SAT is worth approximately ten points. The nineteen Sentence Completion questions contain quite a number of "tough" words whose meanings you will have to know in order to answer these questions correctly.

We must also bring to your attention the fact that several "tough" words show up in the Reading Comprehension passages of every SAT exam. Knowing the meanings of these difficult words will, of course, help you to understand the passages better. It follows that knowing what the passages are about will help you get many more correct answers for the Reading Comprehension questions that appear in the SAT.

Ten Steps to Word Power

1. Study vocabulary lists. This book has just the list you need for SAT preparation. The SAT 2300 Vocabulary Word Review List begins on page 93.

2. Take vocabulary tests. Fifty Vocabulary Practice Tests begin on page 149.

3. Learn those Latin and Greek roots, prefixes, and suffixes that make up many English words. It has been estimated that more than half of all English words come from Latin and Greek. Developing Your Vocabulary Through Prefixes, Roots, and Suffixes That Can Give You the Meaning of over 200,000 Words begins on page 11. Also learn the Hot Prefixes and Roots, page 33.

4. Have a college-level dictionary at home. Carry a pocket dictionary with you. Refer to a dictionary whenever you are not sure of the meaning of a word.

5. Read—read—read. By reading a great deal, you will encounter new and valuable words. You will learn the meanings of many of these words by context—that is, you will perceive a clear connection between a new word and the words that surround that word. In this way, you will learn the meaning of that new word.

6. Listen to what is worthwhile listening to. Listen to good radio and TV programs. Listen to people who speak well. Go to selected movies and plays. Just as you will increase your vocabulary by reading widely, you will increase your vocabulary by listening to English that is spoken well.

7. Play word games like crossword puzzles, anagrams, and Scrabble.

8. Make sure you learn the Vocabulary Strategies beginning on page 47.

9. Study the Most Frequent Positive-Negative SAT Words on page 79.

10. Look at the List of Words Appearing More Than Once on the SAT on page 265.

No One Can Dispute This Fact!

You will pile up SAT points by taking advantage of the valuable Vocabulary Building study and practice materials that are offered to you in the following pages of this chapter.

DIAGNOSTIC
VOCABULARY TEST
WITH ANSWERS

Take this test to find out what strategies you need to increase your vocabulary.

If you get any of these questions wrong, or don't know the answer, look at the explanation and refer to the strategy or page referenced in the answer. You will see other questions related to that strategy or reference.

1. What is the opposite of PRECURSORY?

   A. flamboyant
   B. succeeding
   C. cautious
   D. simple
   E. not planned

2. Which two words do not belong with the others?

   A. fallible
   B. congruous
   C. flammable
   D. famous
   E. exact

3. What is the opposite of EBULLIENT?

   A. aggressive
   B. tranquil
   C. compliant

4. Name words that mean the same as to calm or make better.

5. What is the meaning of ENCROACH?

6. What is the meaning of ELONGATE?

7. Using root meanings, the definition of MANUMIT is:

   A. to manufacture
   B. to be masculine
   C. to set free

Diagnostic Vocabulary Test Answers

1. B—The Gruber list of prefixes, roots, and suffixes can give you the meaning of over 200,000 words. PRE means before; CURS means to run. So PRECURSORY means to run (or go) before. The opposite is running or going *after*, or "succeeding." **Vocabulary Strategy 1** (page 49, Example 9).

2. C and D—If we put the prefix "in" in front of each word, the new word means the opposite of the original word, except for "flammable" ("inflammable" has the same meaning as "flammable") and "famous" ("infamous" has the same meaning as "famous," although "infamous" is "famous" in a bad way). **Latin Prefixes** (page 22).

3. B—Think of "ebullient" as a big-sounding word. The opposite would be "tranquil." **Vocabulary Strategy 2** (page 54).

4. Abate, accede, accommodate, allay, appease, assuage, comply, concede, conciliate, gratify, mitigate, mollify, pacify, placate, propitiate, quell, satiate— **Words That Have the Same Meaning** (page 79).

5. To trespass—**The 2300 Vocabulary Word Review List** (page 93).

6. To make longer or lengthen—Think of the "long" in "elongate." **Vocabulary Strategy 3** (page 59, Example 5).

7. C—MAN means hand; MIT means send. So MANUMIT means to send by hand or to set free. **Latin and Greek Roots** (page 13).

DEVELOPING YOUR VOCABULARY THROUGH PREFIXES, ROOTS, AND SUFFIXES THAT CAN GIVE YOU THE MEANING OF OVER 200,000 WORDS

A Gruber Prefix-Root-Suffix List that Gives You the Meaning of Over 200,000 Words

According to some linguistic studies made, approximately 60 percent of our English words are derived from Latin and Greek. The following Latin and Greek roots, prefixes, and suffixes frequently show up in some of the words that appear in Reading Skills passages. Learn these Latin and Greek word parts to increase your reading vocabulary immensely and thus score well in your Reading Skills test. These prefixes, roots, and suffixes can give you the meaning of over 200,000 words!

Latin and Greek Roots

The shortest and best way of learning a language is to know the roots of it; that is, those original primitive words of which other words are formed.

—Lord Chesterfield

Roots are parts of words that come from other languages—chiefly Latin and Greek. These roots are used as important "building blocks" of many of our English words. As you study the following list of Latin and Greek roots, have a dictionary by your side. Look up the meanings of the word examples that are given with the roots, if you do not know what the word examples mean.

ROOT	MEANING AND EXAMPLE
ag, act	do, drive, act; as *agent*, counter*act*.
alt	high; as *alt*itude, *alt*ar.
anim	mind; as un*anim*ous, *anim*osity.
ann	year; as *ann*als, bie*nn*ial.
aper, apert	open; as *aper*ient, a*pert*ure.
apt	fit, join; as *adapt*.
arch	rule, govern; as an*arch*y.
art	skill; as *art*.
aud	hear, listen; as *aud*ible.
aur	gold; as *aur*iferous (ferr = carry).
bas	low; as de*bas*e.

ROOT	MEANING AND EXAMPLE
bat	beat; as *bat*tle.
bit	bite; as *bite*, *bit*ter.
brev	short; as ab*brev*iate.
cad, cas	fall; as *cad*ence, *cas*ual, ac*cid*ent.
cant	sing; as *cant*icle, *chant*.
cap, capt	take, hold; as *cap*able, *cap*tive.
capit	head; as *capit*al.
carn	flesh; as *carn*ivorous (vor = devour).
ced, cess	go, yield; as ac*cede*, ac*cess*.
celer	swift; as *celer*ity.
cent	hundred; as *cent*ury.
cing, cinet	bind; as sur*cing*le, *cinct*ure, suc*cinct*.
clin	lean, bend; as de*clin*e.
commod	suitable; as *commod*ious.
commun	common; as *commun*ity.
cor, cord	heart; as ac*cord*.
coron	crown; as *coron*ation.
corpus, corpor	body; as *corpu*scle; *corpor*al.
cred	believe; as *cred*ible.
cur	care; as ac*cur*ate.
curr, curs	run; as *curr*ent, *curs*ory.
cycl	circle; as bi*cycl*e.
dat	give; as *dat*e, e*dit*ion.
dent	tooth; as *dent*ist.
di	day; as *di*al.
dict	speak, say; as contra*dict*.
dign	worthy; as *dign*ity, dis*dain*.
domin	lord, master; as *domin*ate.
dorm	sleep; as *dorm*ant.
due, duct	lead, bring; as in*duce*, con*duct*.

ROOT	MEANING AND EXAMPLE
equ	equal; as *equ*animity (anim = mind).
fa	speak; as af*fa*ble.
fac	face, form; as ef*fac*e.
fac, fact	make, form, do; as *fac*ile, *fact*ion.
felic	happy; as *felic*ity.
fer	carry, bear, bring; as *fer*tile, con*fer*.
fess	acknowledge; as con*fess*.
fid	faith, trust; as con*fid*e.
fin	end, limit; as *fin*al.
form	shape; as con*form*.
fort	strong; as *fort*itude.
frag, fract	break; as *frag*ile, *fract*ion.
fund, fus	pour, melt; as *fus*ible, con*found*.
gen, gener	kind, race; as *gen*der, *gener*al.
gest	carry; bring; as con*gest*ion.
grad; gress	step, go; as *grad*ual, di*gress*.
gran	grain; as *gran*ary.
graph	write; as auto*graph*.
grat	pleasing; as *grat*eful.
gross	fat, thick; as *gross*.
hor	hour; as *hor*ology.
hospit	host, guest; as *hospit*able.
integr	entire, whole; as *integr*al.
ject	throw; as in*ject*.
judic	judge; as *judic*iary.
junct	join; as con*junct*ion.
jur	swear; as ad*jur*e.
jur	law, right; as *jur*ist.
lat	carry, bring; as di*lat*e.
leg	send, bring; as *leg*acy, al*leg*e.

ROOT	MEANING AND EXAMPLE
leg, lect	gather, choose; as *leg*ion, ec*lect*ic.
liber	free; as *liber*ty.
lin	flax; as *lin*en, *lin*ing.
lingu	tongue; as *lingu*ist.
liter	letter; as *liter*al; *liter*ary.
loc	place; as *loc*al; dis*loc*ate.
log	word, speech, reason; as cata*log*ue, *log*ic.
loqu, locut	speak, talk; as *loqu*acious, circum*locut*ion.
lud, lus	sport, play; as *lud*icrous, il*lus*ion.
magn	great; as *magn*itude.
major	greater; as *major*ity.
man	hand; as *man*ual, *main*tain.
man, mans	stay, dwell; as *man*or, *mans*ion.
mar	the sea; as *mar*ine.
mater, matr	mother; as *mater*nal, *matr*imony.
medi	middle, between; as *medi*ate.
medic	physician; as *medic*ine.
mens	measure; as *mens*uration.
ment	mind; as *ment*al.
merc	merchandise, trade; as com*merc*e.
merg	dip, sink; as sub*merg*e.
meter; metr	measure; as chrono*meter*, sym*metr*y.
migr	wander; as *migr*ate.
mir	wonder, look; as ad*mir*e, *mir*ror.
mit, miss	send; as ad*mit*, com*miss*ion.
mon, monit	advise, remind; as *mon*ument, *monit*or.
mort	death; as *mort*al.
mot	move; as *mot*or.
mult	many; as *mult*itude.
mun, munit	fortify; as *mun*ition.

ROOT	MEANING AND EXAMPLE
nat	born; as *nat*al.
nav	ship; as *nav*al.
not	known; as *not*ice.
numer	number; as *numer*ous.
nunci, nounce	tell; as e*nunci*ate, an*nounce*.
ocul	eye; as *ocul*ist.
pan	bread; as *pan*try.
par	equal; as dis*par*ity.
par	get ready; as com*par*e.
parl	speak; as *parl*ey.
pars, part	part; as *pars*e, a*part*.
pass	step; as com*pass*.
past	feed; as *past*ure.
pat, pass	suffer, feel; as *pat*ient, *pass*ive.
pater, patr	father; as *pater*nal, *patr*ician.
ped	foot; as bi*ped*.
pell, puls	drive; as com*pel*, ex*puls*ion.
pen	pain, punishment; as *pen*al.
pend, pens	hang, weigh, pay; as *pend*ant, *pens*ion.
pet, petit	seek; as im*pet*us, *petit*ion.
petr	stone, rock; as *petr*ify.
phil, philo	loving; as *philo*sophy (soph = wisdom).
phon	sound; as *phon*ic.
physi	nature; as *physi*ology (log = word, reason).
pict	paint; as *pict*ure.
plac	please; as *plac*able.
ple, plet	fill; as com*ple*ment, com*plet*e.
plen	full; as *plen*ty.
plic	fold, bend; as com*plic*ate.
plum	feather; as *plum*age.

ROOT	MEANING AND EXAMPLE
plumb	lead; as *plumb*er.
pon	to place, put; as com*pon*ent.
port	carry, bring; *port*er.
port	gate; as *port*al.
pos	to place, put; as com*pos*e.
pot	drink; as *pot*ion.
potent	powerful; as *potent*ate.
prehend, prehens	take, grasp; as ap*prehend*, *prehens*ile.
prim	first; as *prim*ary.
punct	prick, point; as *punct*ure.
quadr	square, fourfold; as *quadr*ant.
quant	how much; as *quant*ity.
quer, quisit	seek, ask; as *quer*y, in*quisit*ion.
quies	rest; as ac*quies*ent.
radi	ray; as *radi*ant.
rap, rapt	seize, grasp; as *rap*acious, *rapt*ure.
rat	think, calculate; as *rat*io.
rect	ruled, straight, right; as *rect*angle.
reg	rule, govern; as *reg*ent.
rid, ris	laugh; as *rid*iculous, *ris*ible.
riv	stream; as *riv*er, de*riv*e.
rog, rogat	ask; as inter*rog*ate.
rupt	break; as *rupt*ure.
saer	holy; as *sac*red.
sal	salt; as *sal*ine.
sal	leap; as *sal*ient.
sanct	holy; as *sanct*ion.
sat, satis	enough; as *sat*e, *satis*fy.
sci	know; as *sci*ence.
scop	watch, view; as horo*scop*e.

ROOT	MEANING AND EXAMPLE
scrib, script	write; as de*scribe*, sub*script*ion.
sec, sect	cut; as *sec*ant, bi*sect*.
sen	old; as *sen*ior.
sent, sens	feel, think; as *sent*iment, *sens*ible.
sequ, secut	follow; as *sequ*el, con*secut*ive.
serv	keep; as con*serv*e.
sist	to place, stand; as as*sist*.
sol	alone; as *sol*itude.
son	sound; as con*son*ant.
sort	lot, kind; as as*sort*.
spec, spect	look, appear; as *spec*imen, pro*spect*.
speci	kind; as *speci*es.
spir	breathe; as a*spir*e.
stat	standing; as *stat*us.
stell	star; con*stell*ation.
string, strict	draw tight, bind; as *string*ent.
stru, struct	build; as con*strue*, con*struct*.
su	follow; as pur*su*e.
suad, suas	persuade; as dis*suade*, per*suas*ion.
sum, sumpt	take; as as*sume*, pre*sumpt*ion.
surg, surrect	rise; as in*surg*ent, in*surrect*ion.
tact	touch; as con*tact*.
tail	cut; as *tail*or.
tang	touch; as *tang*ent.
teg, tect	cover; as *teg*ument, de*tect*.
tempor	time; as *tempor*ary.
tend, tent	stretch, reach; as con*tend*, con*tent*.
test	witness; as at*test*.
tort	twist, wring; as con*tort*.
tract	draw; as at*tract*.

ROOT	MEANING AND EXAMPLE
trit	rub; as at*trit*ion.
trud, trus	thrust; as in*trud*e, abs*trus*e.
un	one; as *un*animous (anim = mind).
und	wave, flow; as in*und*ate.
ut, util	use, useful; as *ut*ensil, *util*ize.
vad, vas	go; as e*vad*e.
val	be strong; as *val*id.
ven, vent	come; as con*ven*e, con*vent*ion.
vert, vers	turn; as per*vert*, *vers*ion.
vi, via	way, road; as *vi*aduct (duct = lead, bring), de*vi*ous.
vic	a change, turn; as *vic*arious.
vid, vis	see, appear; as e*vid*ent, *vis*ible.
viv	live; as *viv*acity.
voc	call; as *voc*ation.
volv, volu, volut	roll; as circum*volv*e, *volu*ble, re*volut*ion.
vot	vow; as *vot*ive.

Prefixes and Suffixes

Following is a list of the principal *prefixes* and *suffixes* of Anglo-Saxon (old form of English), Latin, and Greek origin, now in use in the English language:

ENGLISH PREFIXES

Those used to form nouns:

fore	before; as *fore-father*.
mis	wrong; as *mis-deed, mis-chance*.
un	the opposite of; as *un-truth, un-belief.*

Those used to form adjectives:

a	on; as *a-live, a-board, a-sleep*.
for	quite, thoroughly; as *for-lorn*.
un	not; as *un-true, un-wise*.
mis	wrong; as *mis-shapen*.

Those used to form verbs:

a	out, from, away, often used to intensify the meaning of the verb; as *a-rise, a·wake, a-rouse*.
be	by, and is used in several ways:

1. To intensify the meaning of the verb; as *be-daub, be-smear*.
2. To change intransitive verbs to transitive ones; as *be-speak, be-think*.
3. To form transitive verbs out of adjectives and nouns; as *be-friend, be-night, be-troth*.

for	through, thoroughly, used to intensify the meaning of the verb; as *for-bid, for-give, for-get*.
fore	before; as *fore-bode, fore-tell*.
mis	wrongly; as *mis-believe, mis·call*.

un	back; as *un-bind, un-do*.
with	back, against; as *with-draw, with-stand*.

Those used to form adverbs:

a	on; as *a-foot, a-field*.
be	on; as *be-fore, be-sides*.

LATIN PREFIXES

Latin prefixes frequently vary their forms in composition, the final letter being changed to harmonize in sound with the first syllable of the base. Thus, ad becomes ac in *accede*; al in *allude*; at in *attract*; and so on. This process is called assimilation of sound.

The following are the more commonly used prefixes of Latin origin:

a, ab, abs	from, away; as *a-vert, ab-jure, abs-ent*.
ad	to; as *ad-here*. By assimilation *ad* takes the forms *a, ac, af, al, an, ap, as* and *at*, as *a-spire, ac-cord, af-fect, al-lude, an-nex, ap-peal, as-sume, at-tract*.
amb, am (from *ambi*)	about; as *amb-ition, am-putate*.
ante or **anti**	before; as *ante-date, anti-cipate*.
bis, bi	twice; as *bi-sect*.
circum	around; as *circum-navigate*.
com, con	together; as *com-mand, con·vivial*. This prefix assumes the forms *col* and *cor* before *l* and *r* and *co* before a vowel; as *col-lect, cor-rect, com-mit, co-eval, co-worker*.
contra, contro, or **counter**	against; as *contra-dict, contra-vert, counter-act*.
de	down, from, about; as *de-scend, de-part, de-scribe*.
demi	half; as *demi-god*.

dis, di, dif	apart; in two, denoting difference or negation; as *dis-sent, di-vision, dif-ficulty.*
ex, e, or **ef**	out of, from; as *ex-alt, e-lect, ef-face.*
extra	out of, beyond; as *extra-ordinary.*
in	in, into; as *in-vade.* This prefix changes by assimilation into *il, im, ir*; as *il-lustrate, im-merse, ir-ritate.* In its French form, *en*, it is found in *en-chant, en-dure*, etc.
in	not; by assimilation *il, im, ir*; as *in-distinct, il-legal, im-piety, ir-revocable.*
inter, intro	between, within, among; as *inter-pose, intro-duce, enter-prise.*
male	ill; as *mal-treat, male-volent.*
non	not; as *non-sense.*
ob	in front of, against; by assimilation, *oc, of, op*; as *ob-viate, oc-cupy, of-fend, op-pose.*
pene, pen	almost; as *pen-insula.*
per	through; by assimilation, *pel* and *pil*; as *per-ceive, pel-lucid, pil-grim.*
post	after; as *post-pone, post-script.*
pre	before; as *pre-dict, pre-cede.*
preter	past, beyond; as *preter-ite, preter-natural.*
pro	forward, before; as *pro-ceed, pro-gress. Pro* is found in the forms *pur* and *por* in *pur-chase, pur-sue, por-tray.*
pro	instead of; as *pro-noun.*
re, red	back, again; as *re-cede, re-adopt, red-olent.*
retro	backwards; as *retro-grade, retro-spect.*
se, sed	apart, away; as *se-cede, sed-ition.*
semi	half; as *semi-circle.*
sine	without; as *sine-cure.*

sub	under, up from below; by assimilation, *suc, suf, sug, sum, sup, sur, sus;* as *sub-ject, suc-cor, suf-fer, sug-gest, sum-mon, sup-press, sur-prise, sus-tain.*
subter	under; as *subter-fuge.*
super, sur	above, beyond; as *super-pose, super-natural, sur-name.*
trans	across; as *trans-form.*
ultra	beyond; as *ultra-liberal.*
un, uni	one; as *un-animous, uni-form.*
vice	instead of; as *vice-chancellor, vice-roy.*

GREEK PREFIXES

The following are the Greek prefixes in most common use:

a, an	not; as *an-archy, a-morphous.*
amphi	on both sides, round about; as *amphi-bious, amphi-theater.*
ana	up, back; as *ana-tomy, ana-lysis.*
anti	against, opposite to; as *anti-dote, ant-arctic.*
apo, ap	away from; as *apo-state, apo-stle, ap-helion.*
archi, arche, arch	first, chief; as *archi-tect, arche-type, arch-bishop.*
auto, auth	self; as *auto-crat, auto-nomy, auth-entic.*
cata, cat	down, over; as *cata-logue, cat-astrophe.*
dia	through, across; as *dia-meter, dia-gonal.*
dis, di	twice; as *dis-syllable, di-pthong.*
dys	ill; as *dys-peptic.*
ec, ex	out of; as *ec-centric, ex-odus.*
en, el, em	in, all, at; as *en-comium, el-lipse, em-phasis.*

epi	upon; as *epi-taph, epi-demic*.
eu, ev	well; as *eu-logy, ev-angelist*.
hemi	half; as *hemi-sphere*.
hyper	over, above; as *hyper-bole, hyper-critical*.
hypo	under; as *hypo-crite*.
meta, met	after, changed for; as *meta-phor, met-onymy*.
mono	alone; as *mono-gram, mono-poly*.
pan	all; as *pan-acea, pan-orama*.
para, par	beside, against; as *para-dox, par-enthesis*.
peri	around; as *peri-meter, peri-gee, peri-helion*.
poly	many; as *poly-gamy, poly-gon, poly-technic*.
pro	before; as *pro-phet, pro-logue*.
syn, syl, sym, sy	with; as *syn-tax, syl-lable, sym-pathy, sy-stem*.

ENGLISH SUFFIXES

The principal English suffixes are the following:

<u>Those used to form abstract nouns:</u>

dom	denoting judgment, authority, dominion; as *wis-dom, free-dom, king-dom*.
hood, head	denoting state, rank, character; as *man-hood, god-head*.
ing	denoting action, state; as *read-ing, hear-ing*.
ness	denoting state, quality; as *good-ness, great-ness*.
red	denoting mode, fashion; as *hat-red, kind-red*.
ship	denoting shape, manner, form; as *friend-ship, wor-ship = worth-ship*.

<u>Those used to form diminutives:</u>

en	as *maid-en, kitt-en* (from *cat*), *kitch-en* (from *cook*).

ie	as *bird-ie, dog-g-ie, Ann-ie.*
ing	as *farth-ing* (from *fourth*), *tith-ing* (from *tenth*).
kin	as *bump-kin, lamb-kin, nap·kin.*
ling	as *dar-ling, duck-ling, gos-ling.*
ock	as *bull-ock, hill-ock.*

Miscellaneous:

er, ar, or, ier, yer	denoting the agent or doer; as *paint-er, begg-ar, sail-or, cloth-ier, law-yer.*
ster	(formerly a feminine suffix) denoting a female agent; as *spin-ster;* also an agent of either sex; as *huck-ster, poll-ster.* It is also used as a term of depreciation; as *game-ster, young-ster.*
ard, art	characterizing a person by a peculiarity; as *cow-ard, drunk-ard, brag-g-art.*
le, el	denoting an instrument; as *gird-le, hand-le, shov-el.*
ther	marking the agent and used in terms of relationship; as *fa-ther, daugh-ter, mo-ther.*
craft	denoting skill, a trade; as *book-craft, wood-craft.*
fare	denoting way, course; as *thorough-fare, wel-fare.*
ric	denoting power, dominion; as *bishop-ric.*
wright	a workman; as *wheel-wright; play-wright.*
monger	a dealer; as *news-monger.*

Those used to form adjectives:

ed, d	the suffix of the past participle, is added to nouns to form adjectives; as *wing-ed, talent-ed, bright-eye-d, golden-hair-ed.*
en	made of; as *wood-en, gold-en.*
fast	fast, firm; as *stead-fast, shame-faced = shame-fast,* which is the old form of the word.

fold	denoting multiplication; as *two-fold, mani-fold*.
ful	full; as *hate-ful, will-ful*.
ing	the suffix of the present participle; as *pleas-ing, annoy-ing*.
ish	like, when added to nouns; as *boy-ish, girl-ish*; when added to adjectives, the suffix means "somewhat," "rather"; as *black-ish, green-ish*.
less	loose from, without; as *fear-less, shame-less*. This suffix has no connection with the comparative of little.
like	like; as *child-like, war-like*.
ly	like; as *man-ly, sick-ly*. This suffix is a softened form of the preceding.
some	like, partaking of a certain quality; as *glad-some, loath-some*. This suffix is found in a corrupt form in *buxom, flotsam,* and *jetsam*.
teen, ty	ten; as in the numerals.
th	ordinal; as *fif-th, six-th*.
ward	becoming, leading to; as *south-ward, for-ward*.
wise	mode, way, manner; as *like-wise, other-wise*.
y, ey	of the nature of; as *ic-y, show-y*.

Those used to form verbs:

en	imparting the idea of cause, forms transitive verbs from nouns and adjectives; as *strength-en, black-en, fat-t-en*.
er, r	is added to adjectives and verbs, and imparts to the base word a frequentative and intensive force; as *hind-er, low-er, wand-er* (from *wend*), *glimm-er* (from *gleam*).

le, l	is added to nouns and verbs, and imparts to the base word the sense of frequency, or dimunition; as *nest-le, thratt-le* (from *throat*), *start-le, stradd-le* (from *stride*).
k	frequentative; as *tal-k* (from *tell*), *har-k* (from *hear*).
se	to make, forms transitive verbs from adjectives; as *clean-se.*

Those used to form adverbs:

es or s	the old suffix of the possessive case; as in *need-s, beside-s, thence, unawar-es.*
ere	denoting place in; as *here* (related to *he*), *th-ere* (related to *that*), *wh-ere* (related to *who*).
ly	a softened form of like; as *on-ly, utter-ly, wicked-ly.*
ling, long	denoting direction; as in *dark-ling, head-long, side-long.*
ther	denoting place to; as *hi-ther, thi-ther, whi-ther.*
ward, wards	denoting direction; as *home-ward, back-wards.*
wise	mode or manner; as *like-wise, other-wise.*
way, ways	In Old English, the accusative (objective case) of nouns was sometimes used with the force of an adverb. Hence the adverbs *al-ways, straight-way.* The general use of the possessive suffix *-es* or *-s* to form adverbs is accountable for the forms *al-ways, straight-ways, side-ways.*

LATIN SUFFIXES

The principal suffixes of Latin origin are the following:

<u>Those used to form nouns</u>:
1. <u>Those forming abstract nouns</u>:

age	act, condition, collection of; as *cour-age, hom-age, foli-age*.
anee, ancy, ence, or **ency**	state or quality of being; as *abund-ance, const-ancy, indulg-ence, consist-ency*.
ice	that which; as *just-ice*.
ment	state of being, that which; as *excite-ment, command-ment*. It is also used to denote instrument, as in *docu-ment, orna-ment*.
mony	state of, that which; as *acri-mony, resti-mony*.
ion	the act of, state of being; as *redempt-ion, evas-ion, act-ion*.
tude	denoting condition; as *forti-tude, grati-tude*.
ty	state or quality of; as *chari-ty, cruel-ty*.
ure or eur	state of, that which; as *grand-eur, creat-ure*.
y	denoting condition or faculty; as *miser-y, victor-y*.

2. <u>Those denoting simply a person, or one who performs the action signified by the base</u>:

ain or an	connected with; as *artis-an, chapl-ain*.
ant or ent	one who; as *assist-ant, stud-ent*.
ary, ier, eer, or **er**	one who; as *secret-ary, brigad-ier, engin-eer, marin-er*.
ate	one who; as *advoc-ate, cur-ate*. In the French form, *ee* or *e*, this suffix denotes the object of an action; as *legat-ee, nomin-ee, employ-ee*.

ist   one who practises or is devoted to; as *evangel-ist, theor-ist.*

or or **er**   one who; as *conspirat-or, success-or, doct-or, preach-er.*

trix   denoting a female agent; as *execu-trix.*

3. Those forming diminutives:

el or **le**   as *lib-el* (from *liber*, a book), *cast-le* (from *castrum*, a fort).

cle or **cule**   as *vesi-cle, animal-cule.*

ule   as *glob-ule.*

ette or **let**   as *ros-ette, stream-let.*

4. Those forming collective nouns:

ry   as *bandit-ry.*

Those used to form adjectives:

aceous or **acious**   made of, having the quality of; as *farin-aceous, cap-acious.*

al   belonging to; as *leg-al, reg-al.*

an, ane, or **ain**   connected with; as *hum-an, hum-ane, cert-ain.*

ar or **er**   belonging to; as *regul-ar, premi-er.*

ary, arious   relating or belonging to; as *station-ary, greg-arious.*

able or **ible**   that may be done; as *port-able, sens-ible.*

ant or **ent**   equivalent to the force of the present participle inflection -ing; as *discord-ant, cur-rent.*

escent   becoming; as *putr-escent.*

esque   partaking of; as *pictur-esque.*

ic   belonging to; as *civ-ic, rust-ic.*

id   having the quality of; as *acr-id, frig-id.*

ile, il, eel, or **le**   capable of being; as *doc-ile, civ-il, gent-eel, ab-le.*

ine	belonging to; as *can-ine, sal-ine.*
ive	inclined to; as *plaint-ive, abus-ive.*
ory	fitted or relating to; as *admonit-ory.*
ose or **ous**	full of; as *verb-ase, curi-ous.*

<u>Those used to form verbs</u>:

ate	to perform the act of, cause; as *navig-ate.*
fy	to make; as *beauti-fy, magni-fy.*
ish	to make; as *fin-ish.*

GREEK SUFFIXES

ic	belonging to; as *aromat-ic, graph-ic.*
st	agent; as *bapti-st, bolani-st.*
isk	a diminutive; as *aster-isk, obel-isk.*
y	making abstract nouns; as *philosoph-y, monarch-y.*
ize or **ise**	forming verbs; as *anglic-ize, critic-ise.*

THE HOT PREFIXES AND ROOTS THAT DENOTE THE SAME MEANING OR FEELING

Here is a list of the most important prefixes and roots that impart a certain meaning or feeling. They can be instant clues to the meanings of more than 200,000 words.

Prefixes that mean *to*, *with*, *between*, or *among*

PREFIX	MEANING	EXAMPLES
ad, ac, af, an, ap, ap, as, at	to, toward	*adapt*—to fit into *adhere*—to stick to *attract*—to draw near
com, con, co, col	with, together	*combine*—to bring together *contact*—to touch together *collect*—to bring together *co-worker*—one who works together with another worker
in, il, ir, im	into	*inject*—to put into *impose*—to force into *illustrate*—to put into example *irritate*—to put into discomfort
inter	between, among	*international*—among nations *interact*—to act among the people
pro	forward, going ahead	*proceed*—to go forward *promote*—to move forward

Prefixes that mean *bad*

PREFIX	MEANING	EXAMPLES
mal	wrong, bad	*malady*—illness *malevolent*—bad *malfunction*—bad functioning
mis	wrong, badly	*mistreat*—to treat badly *mistake*—to get wrong

Prefixes that mean *away from*, *not*, or *against*

PREFIX	MEANING	EXAMPLES
ab	away from	*absent*—not to be present, away *abscond*—to run away
de, dis	away from, down, the opposite of, apart, not	*depart*—to go away from *decline*—to turn down *dislike*—not to like *dishonest*—not honest *distant*—apart
ex, e, ef	out, from	*exit*—to go out *eject*—to throw out *efface*—to rub out, erase
in, il, ir, im	not	*inactive*—not active *impossible*—not possible *ill-mannered*—not mannered *irreversible*—not reversible
non	not	*nonsense*—no sense *nonstop*—having no stops
un	not	*unhelpful*—not helpful *uninterested*—not interested
anti	against	*anti-freeze*—a substance used to prevent freezing *anti-social*—refers to someone who's not social
ob	against, in front of	*obstacle*—something that stands in the way of *obstinate*—inflexible

Prefixes that denote distance

PREFIX	MEANING	EXAMPLES
circum	around	*circumscribe*—to write or inscribe in a circle *circumspect*—to watch around or be very careful
equ, equi	equal, the same	*equalize*—to make equal *equitable*—fair, equal
post	after	*postpone*—to do after *postmortem*—after death
pre	before	*preview*—a viewing that goes before another viewing *prehistorical*—before written history
trans	across	*transcontinental*—across the continent *transit*—act of going across
re	back, again	*retell*—to tell again *recall*—to call back, to remember
sub	under	*subordinate*—under something else *subconcious*—under the conscious
super	over, above	*superimpose*—to put something over something else *superstar*—a star greater than other stars
un, uni	one	*unity*—oneness *unanimous*—sharing one view *unidirectional*—having one direction

Roots

PREFIX	MEANING	EXAMPLES
cap, capt, cept, ceive	to take, to hold	*captive*—one who is held *receive*—to take *capable*—to be able to take hold of things *concept*—an idea or thought held in mind
cred	to believe	*credible*—believable *credit*—belief, trust
curr, curs, cours	to run	*current*—now in progress, running *cursor*—a moveable indicator *recourse*—to run for aid
dic, dict	to say	*indicate*—to say by demonstrating *diction*—verbal saying
duc, duct	to lead	*induce*—to lead to action *aqueduct*—a pipe or waterway that leads water somewhere
fac, fic, fect, fy	to make, to do	*facile*—easy to do *fiction*—something that has been made up *satisfy*—to make happy *affect*—to make a change in
jec, ject	to throw	*project*—to put forward *trajectory*—a path of an object that has been thrown
mit, mis	to send	*admit*—to send in *missile*—something that gets sent through the air

PREFIX	MEANING	EXAMPLES
pon, pos	to place	*transpose*—to place across *compose*—to put into place many parts *deposit*—to place in something
scrib, script	to write	*describe*—to write or tell about *scripture*—a written tablet
spec, spic	to look	*specimen*—an example to look at *inspect*—to look over
ten, tain	to hold	*maintain*—to hold up or keep *retentive*—holding
ven, vent	to come	*advent*—a coming *convene*—to come together

PREFIX-ROOT-SUFFIX TEST WITH ANSWERS (TEN QUESTIONS)

1. The meaning of TENACIOUS is:

   A. sticking to something
   B. hard to see
   C. terrible
   D. careful

2. The meaning of IRREVERSIBLE is:

   A. not being able to turn back
   B. not being able to understand
   C. careless
   D. being directionless

3. What is the meaning of PRECURSOR?

   A. something that goes before
   B. something that gets someone angry
   C. a careful observation
   D. a hard tool

4. What is the meaning of UNIDIRECTIONAL?

   A. no direction
   B. one direction
   C. many directions
   D. two directions

5. What is the meaning of PARITY?

   A. abundance
   B. simplicity
   C. equality
   D. sympathy

6. What is the meaning of TACTILE?

   A. something that is hard
   B. something that is easy to see
   C. something that can be written on
   D. something that can be touched

7. What is the best meaning of the underlined suffix? *director*

   A. one who
   B. place where
   C. quality of
   D. full of

8. What is the best meaning of the underlined suffix? *anthropology*

    A. being
    B. the quality of
    C. the study of
    D. the place where

9. Which is the prefix of the following word? *inject*

    A. i
    B. in
    C. inj
    D. inject

10. Which is the suffix of *antagonism*?

    A. nism
    B. ism
    C. onism

Prefix-Root-Suffix Test Answers

1. A — TEN = hold fast
2. A — IR = not
3. A — PRE = before, CURS = to run
4. B — UNI = one
5. C — PAR = equal
6. D — TACT = touch
7. A — OR = one who
8. C — OGY = the study of
9. B — Prefix = IN, Root = JECT = to throw
10. B — Suffix = ISM

THREE VOCABULARY STRATEGIES

Introduction

Although **antonyms** (opposites of words) are not on the SAT, it is still important for you to know vocabulary and the strategies to figure out the meanings of words, since there are many questions involving difficult words in all the sections on the Verbal part of the SAT, that is, the **Sentence Completions and Critical Reading Parts**.

VOCABULARY
STRATEGY   1

USE ROOTS, PREFIXES, AND SUFFIXES TO GET THE
MEANINGS OF WORDS

You can increase your vocabulary tremendously by learning Latin and Greek roots, prefixes, and suffixes. Sixty percent of all the words in our English language are derived from Latin and Greek. By learning certain Latin and Greek roots, prefixes, and suffixes, you will be able to understand the meanings of more than 200,000 additional English words. See Developing Your Vocabulary Through Prefixes, Roots, and Suffixes That Can Give You the Meaning of over 200,000 Words on page 11, and The Hot Prefixes and Roots That Denote the Same Meaning or Feeling on page 33.

EXAMPLE 1

Opposite of PROFICIENT:

(A) antiseptic
(B) unwilling
(C) inconsiderate
(D) neglectful
(E) awkward

EXPLANATORY ANSWER

Choice E is correct. The prefix PRO means *forward, for the purpose of.* The root FIC means *to make* or *to do.* Therefore, PROFICIENT literally means *doing something in a forward way.* The definition of *proficient* is *skillful, adept, capable.* The antonym of *proficient* is, accordingly, *awkward, incapable.*

EXAMPLE 2

Opposite of DELUDE:

(A) include
(B) guide
(C) reply
(D) upgrade
(E) welcome

EXPLANATORY ANSWER

Choice B is correct. The prefix DE means *downward, against*. The root LUD means *to play* (a game). Therefore, DELUDE literally means *to play a game against*. The definition of *delude* is *to deceive, to mislead*. The antonym of *delude* is accordingly *to guide*.

EXAMPLE 3

Opposite of LAUDATORY:

(A) vacating
(B) satisfactory
(C) revoking
(D) faultfinding
(E) silent

EXPLANATORY ANSWER

Choice D is correct. The root LAUD means *praise*. The suffix ORY means *a tendency toward*. Therefore, LAUDATORY means having *a tendency toward praising someone*. The definition of *laudatory* is *praising*. The antonym of laudatory is, accordingly, *faultfinding*.

EXAMPLE 4

Opposite of SUBSTANTIATE:

(A) reveal
(B) intimidate
(C) disprove
(D) integrate
(E) assist

EXPLANATORY ANSWER

Choice C is correct. The prefix SUB means *under*. The root STA means *to stand*. The suffix ATE is a verb form indicating *the act of*. Therefore, SUBSTANTIATE literally means *to perform the act of standing under*. The definition of *substantiate* is *to support* with proof or evidence. The antonym is, accordingly, *disprove*.

EXAMPLE 5

Opposite of TENACIOUS:

(A) changing
(B) stupid
(C) unconscious
(D) poor
(E) antagonistic

EXPLANATORY ANSWER

Choice A is correct.
TEN = to hold; TENACIOUS = holding—OPPOSITE = *changing*

EXAMPLE 6

Opposite of RECEDE:

(A) accede
(B) settle
(C) surrender
(D) advance
(E) reform

EXPLANATORY ANSWER

Choice D is correct.
RE = back; CED = to go; RECEDE = to go back—OPPOSITE
= *advance*

EXAMPLE 7

Opposite of CIRCUMSPECT:
(A) suspicious
(B) overbearing
(C) listless
(D) determined
(E) careless

EXPLANATORY ANSWER

Choice E is correct.
CIRCUM = around; SPECT = to look or see; CIRCUMSPECT
= to look all around or make sure that you see everything,
careful—OPPOSITE = *careless*

EXAMPLE 8

Opposite of MALEDICTION:

(A) sloppiness
(B) praise
(C) health
(D) religiousness
(E) proof

EXPLANATORY ANSWER

Choice B is correct.

MAL = bad; DICT = to speak; MALEDICTION = to speak badly about—OPPOSITE = *praise*

EXAMPLE 9

Opposite of PRECURSORY:

(A) succeeding
(B) flamboyant
(C) cautious
(D) simple
(E) cheap

EXPLANATORY ANSWER

Choice A is correct.
PRE = before; CURS = to run; PRECURSORY = run before—OPPOSITE = *succeeding*

EXAMPLE 10

Opposite of CIRCUMVENT:

(A) to go the straight route
(B) alleviate
(C) to prey on one's emotions
(D) scintillate
(E) perceive correctly

EXPLANATORY ANSWER

Choice A is correct.
CIRCUM = around (like a circle); VENT = to come; CIRCUMVENT = to come around—OPPOSITE = *to go the straight route*

PAY ATTENTION TO THE SOUND OR FEELING OF
THE WORD—WHETHER POSITIVE OR NEGATIVE,
HARSH OR MILD, BIG OR LITTLE, ETC.

If the word sounds harsh or terrible, such as "obstreperous," the meaning probably is something harsh or terrible. If you're looking for a word opposite in meaning to "obstreperous," look for a word or words that have a softer sound, such as "pleasantly quiet or docile." The sense of "obstreperous" can also seem to be negative—so if you're looking for a synonym, look for a negative word. If you're looking for an opposite (antonym), look for a positive word.

EXAMPLE 1

Opposite of BELLIGERENCY:

(A) pain
(B) silence
(C) homeliness
(D) elegance
(E) peace

EXPLANATORY ANSWER

Choice E is correct. The word BELLIGERENCY imparts a tone of forcefulness or confusion and means warlike. The opposite would be calmness or peacefulness. The closest choices are choice B or E, with E a little closer to the opposite in tone for the capitalized word. Of course, if you knew the root BELLI means "war," you could see the opposite as (E) peace.

EXAMPLE 2

Opposite of DEGRADE:

(A) startle
(B) elevate
(C) encircle
(D) replace
(E) assemble

EXPLANATORY ANSWER

Choice B is correct. Here you can think of the DE in DEGRADE as a prefix that is negative (bad) and means *down*, and in fact DEGRADE does mean to debase or lower. So you should look for an opposite that would be a word with a *positive* (good) meaning. The best word from the choices is (B) elevate.

EXAMPLE 3

Opposite of OBFUSCATION:

(A) illumination
(B) irritation
(C) conviction
(D) minor offense
(E) stable environment

EXPLANATORY ANSWER

Choice A is correct. The prefix OB is usually negative, as in obstacle or obliterate, and in fact OBFUSCATE means *darken* or *obscure*. So since we are looking for an opposite, you would look for a *positive* word. Choices A and E are positive, and you should go for the more positive of the two, which is Choice A.

EXAMPLE 4

Opposite of MUNIFICENCE:

(A) disloyalty
(B) stinginess
(C) dispersion
(D) simplicity
(E) vehemence

EXPLANATORY ANSWER

Choice B is correct because MUNIFICENCE means *generosity*. Many of the words ending in ENCE, like OPULENCE, EFFERVESCENCE, LUMINESCENCE, QUINTESSENCE, etc., represent or describe something big or bright. So the opposite of one of these words would denote something small or dark.

You can associate the prefix MUNI with money, as in "municipal bonds," so the word MUNIFICENCE must deal with money and in a big way. The opposite deals with money in a small way. Choice B fits the bill.

EXAMPLE 5

Opposite of DETRIMENT:

(A) recurrence
(B) disclosure
(C) resemblance
(D) enhancement
(E) postponement

EXPLANATORY ANSWER

Choice D is correct. The prefix DE can also mean *against* and is negative, and DETRIMENT means something that causes damage or loss. So you should look for a positive word. The only one is (D) enhancement.

EXAMPLE 6

Opposite of UNDERSTATE:

(A) embroider
(B) initiate
(C) distort
(D) pacify
(E) reiterate

EXPLANATORY ANSWER

Choice A is correct. UNDERSTATE means something said in a restrained or downplayed manner. You see "under" in UNDERSTATE so look for a choice that gives you the impression of something that is "over" as in "over-stated." The only choice is (A) embroider, which means *to embellish*.

EXAMPLE 7

Opposite of DISHEARTEN:
(A) engage
(B) encourage
(C) predict
(D) dismember
(E) misinform

EXPLANATORY ANSWER

Choice B is correct. You see "heart" in DISHEARTEN. The DIS is negative or means "not to," or "not to have heart," and dishearten does mean *to discourage*. So you want to look for a *positive* word. Choice (B) encourage fits the bill.

EXAMPLE 8

Opposite of FIREBRAND:

(A) an intellect
(B) one who is charitable
(C) one who makes peace
(D) a philanthropist
(E) one who is dishonest

EXPLANATORY ANSWER

Choice C is correct. You see fire in FIREBRAND. So think of something fiery or dangerous. The opposite of FIREBRAND must be something that's calm or safe. The best choice is Choice C, whereas a FIREBRAND is someone who causes trouble.

USE WORD ASSOCIATIONS TO DETERMINE WORD MEANINGS AND THEIR OPPOSITES

Looking at the root or part of any capitalized word may suggest an association with another word that looks similar and whose meaning you know. This new word's meaning may give you a clue as to the meaning of the original word or the opposite in meaning to the original word if you need an opposite. For example, *extricate* reminds us of the word "extract," the opposite of which is "to put together."

EXAMPLE 1

Opposite of STASIS:

(A) stoppage
(B) reduction
(C) depletion
(D) fluctuation
(E) completion

EXPLANATORY ANSWER

Choice D is correct. Think of STATIC or STATIONARY. The opposite would be moving or fluctuating since STASIS means stopping or retarding movement.

EXAMPLE 2

Opposite of APPEASE:

(A) criticize
(B) analyze
(C) correct
(D) incense
(E) develop

EXPLANATORY ANSWER

Choice D is correct. Appease means to placate. Think of PEACE in APPEASE. The opposite would be violent or incense.

EXAMPLE 3

Opposite of COMMISERATION:
(A) undeserved reward
(B) lack of sympathy
(C) unexpected success
(D) absence of talent
(E) inexplicable danger

EXPLANATORY ANSWER

Choice B is correct. Think of MISERY in the word COMMISERATION. Commiseration means the sharing of misery. Choice B is the only appropriate choice.

EXAMPLE 4

Opposite of JOCULAR:

(A) unintentional
(B) exotic
(C) muscular
(D) exaggerated
(E) serious

EXPLANATORY ANSWER

Choice E is correct. Think of JOKE in the word JOCULAR, which means given to joking. The opposite would be serious.

EXAMPLE 5

Opposite of ELONGATE:

(A) melt
(B) wind
(C) confuse
(D) smooth
(E) shorten

EXPLANATORY ANSWER

Choice E is correct. Think of the word LONG in ELONGATE, which means to lengthen. The opposite would be short or shorten.

EXAMPLE 6

Opposite of SLOTHFUL:

(A) permanent
(B) ambitious
(C) average
(D) truthful
(E) plentiful

EXPLANATORY ANSWER

Choice B is correct. Think of SLOTH, a very, very slow animal. So SLOTHFUL, which means lazy or sluggish, must be slow and unambitious. The opposite would be ambitious.

EXAMPLE 7

Opposite of FORTITUDE:

(A) timidity
(B) conservatism
(C) placidity
(D) laxness
(E) ambition

EXPLANATORY ANSWER

Choice A is correct. FORTITUDE means strength in the face of adversity; you should think of FORT or FORTIFY as something strong. The opposite would be weakness or *timidity*.

EXAMPLE 8

Opposite of LUCID:

(A) underlying
(B) abstruse
(C) luxurious
(D) tight
(E) general

EXPLANATORY ANSWER

Choice B is correct. LUCID means easily understood or clear; you should think of LUCITE, a clear plastic. The opposite of clear is hard to see through or abstruse. *Note:* The "ab" in "abstruse" makes Choice B the only *negative* choice, which is the opposite of the positive word LUCID.

EXAMPLE 9

Opposite of POTENT:

(A) imposing
(B) pertinent
(C) feeble
(D) comparable
(E) frantic

EXPLANATORY ANSWER

Choice C is correct. Think of the word POTENTIAL or POWERFUL. To have potential is to have the ability or power to be able to do something. So the opposite would be feeble. You could also have thought of POTENT as a *positive* word. The opposite would be a negative word. The only two choices that are negative are choices C and E.

PRACTICE USING THE FIFTY GRUBER PREFIXES AND ROOTS

Roots

ROOT 1

EMISSARY: (A) a statue that is on a pedestal
            (B) a person who travels to see new places
            (C) a messenger sent to represent another person

(C) Remember the root MIS means <u>to send</u>. EMISSARY is a messenger sending (or representing) concerns of another person.

ROOT 2

ASCRIBE: (A) to cancel
           (B) to assign
           (C) to fulfill

(B) Remember SCRIB is the root that means <u>to write</u>. So ASCRIBE means to write on or, less literally, to assign.

ROOT 3

EXTANT: (A) still in existence
          (B) far off into space
          (C) something drawn between two parallel lines

(A) Remember the root STA means <u>to stand</u>. In this case the X in EXTANT can be thought of as an S creating the root STA. EXTANT means to stand or, less literally, still be in existence.

ROOT 4

OFFICIOUS: (A) paying attention to the rules
             (B) eager to render service
             (C) aspiring to a higher position

(B) The root FIC means <u>to make or to do</u>. The word OFFICIOUS means eager to do service.

ROOT 5

VOCIFEROUS: (A) making an outcry
                    (B) constantly seeking employment
                    (C) bringing disease

(A) The root FER means to carry or bear. The root VOC means voice as in VOCAL. So the word VOCIFEROUS means to carry a voice or, less literally, to make an outcry.

ROOT 6

TENET: (A) A structure that covers a large area
                (B) An assumption made in a scientific discipline
                (C) A principle held by an organization

(C) The root TEN means to hold. TENET is a principle held by an organization.

IMPORTANT:

Many times the root or prefix of a word can immediately give you the meaning of the word without you having to do deeper analysis. This is useful on tests where you may be able to zero in on the right choice by spotting the prefix or root of the word and matching it with one of the choices.

For example: Find the OPPOSITE of the meaning of PRECURSORY:

(A) succeeding (B) creative (C) speeding

If you know that the prefix PRE means before, you don't even have to know what the root CURS means to see that the opposite of PRE means after, signalling choice A.

These prefixes and roots are a passport to not only quickly seeing what the meaning of a word is, but also enabling you to perform far better on standardized vocabulary tests by zeroing in on the correct choice or eliminating the incorrect ones.

ROOT 7

REPOSE: (A) state of occurring again
(B) state of being in an angry mood
(C) state of being at rest

(C) The root POS means <u>to put or to place</u>. REPOSE means the state of placing or putting at rest.

ROOT 8

ADDUCE: (A) to bring forward for consideration
(B) to understand thoroughly
(C) to count up many times

(A) The root DUC means <u>to lead</u>. The word ADDUCE means bring forward for consideration.

ROOT 9

PORTENTOUS: (A) illustrative
(B) foreboding
(C) very strict

(B) The root TENT means <u>to stretch</u>. The prefix POR (used instead of PRO) means <u>forward</u>. So PORTENTOUS means stretching forward or predicting what is going to happen as in foreboding.

ROOT 10

INTERCEPT: (A) to interrupt
(B) to concede
(C) to push forward

(A) The root CEPT means <u>to take or to seize</u>. INTERCEPT means to seize the continuation or to <u>interrupt</u>.

ROOT 11

REPLICATE: (A) to extract
(B) to duplicate
(C) to initiate

(B) The root PLIC means to fold. The prefix RE means again.

The word REPLICATE means to fold again, or to duplicate.

ROOT 12

CIRCUMSPECT: (A) superficial
(B) antagonistic
(C) prudent

(C) The root SPEC means to look at or to see. The prefix CIRCUM means around. So CIRCUMSPECT means to look around or, less literally, to be careful or prudent.

ROOT 13

CONTROVERT: (A) to deny
(B) to move from one place to another
(C) to stop production

(A) The root VERT means to turn. The prefix CONTR means against. So CONTROVERT means to turn against or to deny.

ROOT 14

CEDE: (A) to yield
(B) to plant
(C) to grow

(A) The root CED means to yield, so CEDE means simply to yield.

ROOT 15

AGITATE: (A) to conform
                          (B) to style
                          (C) to excite

(C) The root AG means <u>to do or to act</u>. AGITATE means to excite.

ROOT 16

CURSOR: (A) a vulgar person
                          (B) a sharp edge
                          (C) a running marker

(C) The root CURS means <u>to run</u>. A CURSOR is the running marker on the computer. So that's where the term comes from!

ROOT 17

INDICT: (A) to accuse
                          (B) to refer to
                          (C) to cease

(A) The root DICT means <u>to say</u>. The prefix IN means in. INDICT means to accuse.

ROOT 18

CONJECTURE: (A) to fortell
                          (B) to grasp
                          (C) to guess

(C) The root JECT means <u>to throw</u>. The prefix CON means <u>with</u>. CONJECTURE means "with throwing" or, less literally, to guess.

ROOT 19

BENEDICTION: (A) a blessing
(B) a calm statement
(C) a religious painting

(A) The root (also prefix) BENE means <u>good</u>. The root DICT means <u>to say</u>. So BENEDICTION means something good that is said, or a blessing.

ROOT 20

PROGENY: (A) children or offspring
(B) substances with chemical or biological similarities
(C) a creative or inventive procedure

(A) The root GEN means <u>born</u>. The prefix PRO means <u>forward</u>. The word PROGENY means children or offspring.

Prefixes

PREFIX 1

ABDICATE: (A) to say terrible things about someone
                          (B) to relinquish power
                          (C) to destroy

(B) The prefix AB means <u>away from</u>. The root DIC means <u>to say</u>. ABDICATE means to relinquish power.

PREFIX 2

ADVERT: (A) to stop motion
                          (B) to call attention to
                          (C) to adjust oneself to

(B) The prefix AD means <u>to</u>. The root VERT means <u>turn</u>. ADVERT means turn to or call attention to.

PREFIX 3

COLLOCATE: (A) to arrange
                          (B) to liquidate
                          (C) to liquify

(A) The prefix COL means <u>with</u> or <u>together</u>. The root LOC means <u>location</u>. COLLOCATE is a "location together" or means to arrange.

PREFIX 4

DECLIVITY: (A) a sharp edge
                          (B) a peak
                          (C) a descending slope

(C) The prefix DE means <u>down</u>. CLI is derived from <u>climb</u> or <u>slope</u>.

So DECLIVITY is a downward or descending slope. ACCLIVITY is an upward or rising slope because AC means <u>up</u>.

PREFIX 5

DIFFIDENT: (A) supportive
                (B) finicky
                (C) not confident

(C) The prefix DI means <u>away from</u> or <u>apart</u>. The root FID means <u>trust</u>. So DIFFIDENT is not trusting or not confident. Notice that because CON means <u>with</u>, the word CONFIDENT gets its meaning using CON and FID as the prefix and root.

PREFIX 6

DISPARAGE: (A) to modify
                (B) to take apart
                (C) to belittle

(C) The prefix DIS means <u>not</u>. PARAGE means <u>rank</u>. So DISPARAGE is not to rank or to belittle.

PREFIX 7

ELOCUTION: (A) the style of speaking
                (B) the manner of dress
                (C) the high point on a building

(A) The prefix E means <u>out</u> or <u>from</u>. The root LOCUT means <u>speak</u>. So ELOCUTION means speaking from or the style of speaking.

PREFIX 8

INTERPOLATE: (A) to insert or introduce between two other items
                (B) to create a state of calmness or peacefulness
                (C) to judge according to a set of given rules

(A) The prefix INTER means <u>between</u>. INTERPOLATE means to insert or introduce between two other items or things.

PREFIX 9

MISCREANT: (A) a wanderer
                  (B) an uneducated worker
                  (C) a villain

(C) The prefix MIS means wrongly or badly. MISCREANT is a bad person or villain.

PREFIX 10

NONCHALANT: (A) adorned
                  (B) peasantlike
                  (C) indifferent

(C) The prefix NON means not. NONCHALANT means not caring or indifferent.

PREFIX 11

OBVIATE: (A) prevent
                  (B) make known
                  (C) start up

(A) The prefix OB means in the way or against. OBVIATE means to prevent or dispose of.

PREFIX 12

PROLIFEROUS: (A) standing out
                  (B) reproducing freely
                  (C) extremely agile

(B) The prefix PRO means forward. The root FER means to carry or to bear. PROLIFEROUS means reproducing freely.

PREFIX 13

PREPENSE: (A) arranged in advance
                    (B) a specified amount of money
                    (C) the judgment after a trial

(A) The prefix PRE means <u>before</u>. The root PENS means <u>thought</u>. So PREPENSE is thought before or arranged in advance.

PREFIX 14

REPUDIATION: (A) trying to invalidate something
                    (B) setting a standard of quality
                    (C) showing fear or concern

(A) The prefix RE means <u>back</u> or <u>again</u>. REPUDIATION is the act of trying to take back the truth of something or invalidating something.

PREFIX 15

SUBSERVIENT: (A) underground
                    (B) lower than others in function
                    (C) an assistant

(B) The prefix SUB means <u>under</u>. Think of SERV from service. So SUBSERVIENT means lower than others in capacity or function.

PREFIX 16

SUPERFLUOUS: (A) floating to the surface
                    (B) beyond what is required
                    (C) infinite in wisdom

(B) The prefix SUPER means <u>beyond</u> or <u>over</u>. SUPERFLUOUS means beyond what is required—something a lot more than you need.

PREFIX 17

TRANSVERSE: (A) unified
                 (B) unstable
                 (C) lying across

(C) The prefix TRANS means across. TRANSVERSE means lying across.

PREFIX 18

IMMISCIBLE: (A) not able to be mixed
                (B) not able to be seen through
                (C) definite and sharp

(A) The prefix IM, in this case, means not. Think of MIS as mix, so IMMISCIBLE means not able to be mixed.

PREFIX 19

MONODY: (A) a boring person
              (B) an ode for one voice or actor
              (C) a conglomerate of buildings

(B) The prefix MONO means one. MONODY is an ode (OD in MONODY) for one voice or actor.

PREFIX 20

BIPARTITE: (A) a group of dissidents
               (B) a country at war
               (C) having two parts

(C) The prefix BI means two. BIPARTITE means having two parts.

PREFIX 21

ANTITHETICAL: (A) hypothetical
                  (B) against religion of any form
                  (C) opposed in every respect

(C) The prefix ANTI means against. ANTITHETICAL means opposed in every respect.

PREFIX 22

CIRCUMVENT: (A) to avoid
                   (B) to open
                   (C) to watch in a careful manner

(A) The prefix CIRCUM means <u>around</u> as in CIRCLE. The root VEN means <u>to come</u>. CIRCUMVENT means to avoid as if by coming around.

PREFIX 23

EQUANIMITY: (A) having equal lengths or sides
                   (B) calm or even-tempered
                   (C) having the same rank or status

(B) The prefix EQU means <u>equal</u>. ANIM refers to <u>a person or animal</u>. EQUANIMITY means calm or even(equal)-tempered.

PREFIX 24

MALAPROPISM: (A) a faulty set on a stage
                    (B) a trite remark or cliche
                    (C) a misuse of a word

(C) The prefix MAL means <u>bad</u>. MALAPROPISM is a misuse of a word.

PREFIX 25

INDUCTION: (A) leading by influence
                 (B) electrical stimulation
                 (C) a prior knowledge of something

(A) The prefix IN, in this case, means <u>in</u> or <u>into</u>. The root DUC means <u>to lead</u>. So INDUCTION means leading into or leading by influence.

PREFIX 26

UNILOCULAR: (A) having a single compartment
                  (B) having only one way to exit
                  (C) completely locked in

(A) The prefix UNI means <u>one</u>. The root LOC means <u>location</u> or <u>place</u>. UNILOCULAR means having a single place or compartment.

PREFIX 27

OMNIFARIOUS: (A) extremely loud
                 (B) completely trustworthy
                 (C) of all kinds

(C) The prefix OMNI means all. OMNIFARIOUS means of all kinds.

PREFIX 28

POLYGLOT: (A) composed of several languages
                 (B) a giant mythical character
                 (C) a medical term for a large cut

(A) The prefix POLY means many. The root GLOT means tongue. So POLYGLOT means many tongues or, less literally, composed of several languages.

PREFIX 29

PERISTYLE: (A) a simple construction
                 (B) an enclosed courtyard
                 (C) a type of calligraphy

(B) The prefix PERI means around as in PERIMETER. PERISTYLE is a style of construction which goes all around to enclose an area, an enclosed courtyard.

PREFIX 30

POSTNATAL: (A) pertaining to the common cold
                 (B) the score one receives after taking an exam
                 (C) occurring immediately after birth

(C) The prefix POST means after. The root NAT means birth as in NATIVITY. POSTNATAL means occurring immediately after birth.

THE MOST FREQUENT POSITIVE-NEGATIVE SAT WORDS— WORDS THAT HAVE THE SAME MEANING; PRACTICE QUESTIONS WITH ANSWERS

Following is a list of popular SAT words and their opposites. *Note:* These words fit into specific categories, and it may be a little easier memorizing the meaning of these important words knowing what category they fit into.

POSITIVE	NEGATIVE
TO PRAISE	TO BELITTLE
acclaim	admonish
applaud	assail
commend	berate
eulogize	calumniate
exalt	castigate
extol	censure
flatter	chastise
hail	chide
laud	decry
panegyrize	denigrate
resound	denounce
tout	disparage
	excoriate
	execrate
	flay
	lambaste
	malign
	reprimand
	reproach
	scold
	upbraid
	vilify

POSITIVE	NEGATIVE
TO CALM OR MAKE BETTER	TO MAKE WORSE OR RUFFLE
abate	alienate
accede	antagonize
accommodate	contradict
allay	dispute
ameliorate	fend off
appease	embitter
assuage	estrange
comply	incense
concede	infuriate
conciliate	nettle
gratify	oppugn
mitigate	oppose
mollify	rebuff
pacify	repel
palliate	repulse
placate	snub
propitiate	
quell	
satiate	

POSITIVE	NEGATIVE
PLEASANT	UNPLEASANT
affable	callous
amiable	cantankerous
agreeable	captious
captivating	churlish
congenial	contentious
cordial	gruff
courteous	irascible
decorous	ireful
engaging	obstinate
gracious	ornery
obliging	peevish
sportive	perverse
unblemished	petulant
undefiled	querulous
	testy
	vexing
	wayward

POSITIVE	NEGATIVE
GENEROUS	CHEAP
altruistic	frugal
beneficent	miserly
benevolent	niggardly
charitable	paltry
effusive	parsimonious
hospitable	penurious
humanitarian	provident
magnanimous	skinflinty
munificent	spartan
philanthropic	tight-fisted
	thrifty

POSITIVE	NEGATIVE
ABUNDANT OR RICH	SCARCE OR POOR
affluent	dearth
bounteous	deficit
copious	destitute
luxuriant	exiguous
multifarious	impecunious
multitudinous	impoverished
myriad	indigent
opulent	insolvent
pecunious	meager
plenteous	paltry
plentiful	paucity
plethoric	penurious
profuse	scanty
prosperous	scarcity
superabundant	sparse
teeming	
wealthy	

POSITIVE	NEGATIVE
YIELDING	NOT YIELDING
accommodating	adamant
amenable	determinate
compliant	immutable
deferential	indomitable
docile	inflexible
flexible	intractable
hospitable	intransigent
inclined	recalcitrant
malleable	relentless
obliging	resolute
pliant	steadfast
submissive	tenacious
subservient	
tractable	

POSITIVE	NEGATIVE
COURAGEOUS	TIMID
audacious	diffident
dauntless	indisposed
gallant	laconic
intrepid	reserved
stalwart	reticent
undaunted	subdued
valiant	timorous
valorous	
LIVELY	BLEAK
brisk	dejected
dynamic	forlorn
ebullient	lackluster
exhilaration	lugubrious
exuberant	melancholy
inspiring	muted
provocative	prostrate
scintillating	somber
stimulating	tenebrous
titillating	

POSITIVE	NEGATIVE
CAREFUL	CARELESS
chary	culpable
circumspect	felonious
conscientious	indifferent
discreet	insouciant
exacting	lackadaisical
fastidious	lax
gingerly	negligent
heedful	perfunctory
judicious	rash
meticulous	remiss
provident	reprehensible
prudent	temerarious
punctilious	
scrupulous	
scrutiny	
wary	

POSITIVE	NEGATIVE
HUMBLE	HAUGHTY
demure	affected
diffident	aristocratic
indisposed	arrogant
introverted	audacious
laconic	authoritarian
plebian	autocratic
reluctant	condescending
restrained	disdainful
reticent	egotistical
subdued	flagrant
subservient	flippant
taciturn	imperious
timid	impertinent
timorous	impudent
unassuming	insolent
unostentatious	ostentatious
unpretentious	pompous
	proud
	supercilious
	vainglorious

Note: In many cases you can put a prefix "im" or "un" in front of the word and change its meaning to an opposite.

Example: Pecunious. Opposite: Impecunious
　　　　Ostentatious. Opposite: Unostentatious

Practice Questions

1. Example: Find OPPOSITE of EXTOL:

   (A) oppose
   (B) restrain
   (C) enter
   (D) deviate
   (E) denigrate

2. ALLAY (opposite):

   (A) incense
   (B) drive
   (C) berate
   (D) signify
   (E) determine

3. DECOROUS (opposite):

   (A) scanty
   (B) irascible
   (C) musty
   (D) pliant
   (E) rigid

4. AMENABLE (opposite):

   (A) tiresome
   (B) uncultured
   (C) intransigent
   (D) soothing
   (E) careless

5. MUNIFICENT (opposite):

   (A) simple
   (B) pallid
   (C) crafty
   (D) penurious
   (E) stable

6. PLETHORIC (opposite):

   (A) impecunious
   (B) slothful
   (C) indifferent
   (D) reticent
   (E) sly

7. METICULOUS (opposite):

   (A) timid
   (B) plenteous
   (C) peevish
   (D) intractable
   (E) perfunctory

8. IMPERIOUS (opposite):

   (A) unostentatious
   (B) lackadaisical
   (C) insolvent
   (D) churlish
   (E) immutable

9. TIMOROUS (opposite):

   (A) judicious
   (B) intrepid
   (C) multifarious
   (D) benevolent
   (E) tenebrous

10. LUGUBRIOUS (opposite):

    (A) flexible
    (B) unblemished
    (C) ebullient
    (D) conciliatory
    (E) impertinent

Answers to Practice Questions

1. Choice E is correct. EXTOL fits into the category of TO PRAISE.
    Denigrate fits into the category TO BELITTLE—the opposite category.

2. Choice A is correct. ALLAY fits into the category of TO CALM. Incense
    fits into the opposite category— TO MAKE WORSE or TO RUFFLE.

3. Choice B is correct. DECOROUS fits into the category of PLEASANT.
    The opposite category is UNPLEASANT. Irascible fits into this category.

4. Choice C is correct. AMENABLE fits into the category of YIELDING.
    Intransigent fits into the opposite category—NOT YIELDING.

5. Choice D is correct. MUNIFICENT fits into the category of
    GENEROUS. Penurious fits into the category of CHEAP, the opposite
    category.

6. Choice A is correct. PLETHORIC fits into the category of
    ABUNDANT or RICH. Impecunious fits into the opposite category of
    SCARCE or POOR.

7. Choice E is correct. METICULOUS fits into the category of CAREFUL.
    Perfunctory fits into the category of CARELESS (or mechanical).

8. Choice A is correct. IMPERIOUS fits into the category of HAUGHTY
    (high-brow). Unostentatious fits into the category of HUMBLE, the
    opposite category.

9. Choice B is correct. TIMOROUS fits into the category of TIMID.
    Intrepid fits into the opposite category of COURAGEOUS.

10. Choice C is correct. LUGUBRIOUS fits into the category of BLEAK or
    dismal. Ebullient fits into the opposite category of LIVELY.

THE 2300 VOCABULARY
WORD REVIEW LIST

A

abase—to degrade

abash—to embarrass

abate—to decrease

abattoir—a slaughterhouse

abdicate—to give up

aberration—a deviation

abet—to aid

abeyance—temporary suspension

abhor—to detest

abject—miserable

abjure—to give up on oath

ablution—washing the body

abnegate—to renounce

abominate—to loathe

aboriginal—first; existing
   someplace since the beginning

abort—to cut short

abrade—to rub off

abridge—to shorten

abrogate—to cancel by authority

abscond—to run away

absolve—to free of guilt

abstemious—moderate in eating
   and drinking

abstract—a summary

abstruse—hard to understand

abut—to border on

abysmal—bottomless; wretched

accede—to take on the duties (of);
   to attain (to)

acclivity—an upward slope

accolade—a demonstration
   of honor

accoutrements—one's clothes

accretion—accumulation

accrue—to accumulate

acerbity—sharpness

acme—a peak

acquiesce—to yield

acquit—to clear of a charge

acrid—sharp

acrimony—bitterness

actuate—to put into motion

acumen—keenness

adage—an old saying

adamant—unyielding

adduce—to give as proof

adept—skilled; expert

adhere—to stay fast

adipose—fatty

adjudicate—to judge

adjunct—something added

adjure—to charge under oath

admonish—to warn

adroit—skillful

adulation—flattery

adulterate—to make impure

adumbration—a foreshadowing;
   an outlining

advent—an arrival

adventitious—accidental

adversity—misfortune

advocate—to support

aesthetic—pertaining to beauty

affable—friendly

affected—artificial

affidavit—a sworn statement
in writing

affinity—a close relationship

affirmation—assertion

affluent—wealthy

affray—a noisy quarrel

affront—an insult

agenda—a program

agglomerate—to gather into a mass

aggrandize—to make greater

aggravate—to make worse

aggregate—a group of things
together

aggrieved—wronged

aghast—horrified

agile—nimble

agnostic—one who doesn't know

agrarian—agricultural

akimbo—with hands on hips

alacrity—eagerness

albeit—although

alchemy—early chemistry

alienate—to make unfriendly

allay—to calm

allege—to declare

allegory—a symbolic story

alleviate—to relieve

allocate—to distribute

allude—to refer indirectly

alluvial—pertaining to soil deposits
left by water

altercation—an angry argument

altruism—unselfish concern
for others

amass—to accumulate

amatory—showing love

ambidextrous—skillful; able to use
both hands equally well

ambrosia—the food of the gods

ambulant—moving about

ameliorate—to improve

amenable—easily led

amenity—a pleasant quality

amiable—friendly

amity—friendship

amnesty—pardon

amorphous—shapeless

amplify—to increase

amulet—a charm

anachronism—something
misplaced in time

analgesic—a pain reliever

analogous—comparable

anarchy—absence of government

anathema—a curse

anchorite—a recluse

ancillary—serving as an aid

animadversion—a critical comment

animate—to bring to life

animosity—hatred

annals—yearly records

anneal—to heat and then cool;
to strengthen

annuity—a yearly payment

annul—to invalidate

anomaly—an abnormality

antediluvian—before the Biblical
flood; very old

anterior—toward the front

anthropoid—resembling man

antipathy—a strong dislike

antipodes—exact opposites

antithesis—opposite

apathetic—indifferent

aperture—an opening

apex—a peak

aphorism—an adage

aplomb—self-possession; poise

apocryphal—of doubtful authenticity

apogee—the highest point

apoplexy—sudden paralysis

apostate—one who abandons his
faith or cause

apothecary—druggist

apothegm—a saying

apotheosis—deification

appall—to shock or dismay

apparition—a ghost

appease—to pacify

appellation—a name or title

append—to attach

apposite—apt

apprise—to notify

appurtenance—an accessory
or possession

aquiline—curved or hooked

arabesque—an elaborate
architectural design

arable—plowable (land)

arbiter—a judge or umpire

arbitrary—left to one's judgment;
despotic

arboreal—pertaining to trees

archaic—ancient or old-fashioned

archetype—an original model or
perfect example

archipelago—a group of islands

archives—a place where records
are kept; records

ardor—passion

arduous—laborious

argot—jargon

armada—a fleet of warships

arraign—to bring to court to
answer charges

arrant—complete; out-and-out

arrears—unpaid debts

arrogate—to appropriate

articulate—to join; to speak clearly

artifact—a manmade object, particularly a primitive one

artifice—ingenuity; trickery

artisan—a skilled craftsman

ascendant—rising

ascetic—self-denying

ascribe—to assign or attribute

aseptic—free of bacteria

askance—with a sideways look; suspiciously

askew—crookedly

asperity—harshness

aspersion—a slanderous remark

assail—to assault

assay—to test or analyze; to try

asseverate—to assert

assiduous—diligent

assimilate—to incorporate

assuage—to lessen

astral—pertaining to the stars

astute—clever; shrewd

atavism—a throwback to an earlier state; a reappearance of a characteristic from an earlier generation

atheist—one who believes there is no God

athwart—across

atrophy—to waste away

attenuate—to weaken

attest—to confirm

attribute—a characteristic

attrition—wearing away

atypical—abnormal

audacious—bold

audible—loud enough to be heard

augment—to enlarge

augur—to foretell

august—inspiring reverence and respect

aural—pertaining to the ear or hearing

auspices—sponsorship

auspicious—favorable

austerity—severity; the condition of denying oneself

autocrat—a dictator

autonomy—self-government; independence

auxiliary—a thing or person that gives aid

avarice—greed

aver—to affirm

averse—opposed

avid—greedy

avocation—a hobby

avoirdupois—weight

avow—to acknowledge

avuncular—pertaining to an uncle; like an uncle

awry—not straight

B

bacchanal—a drunken party

badger—to tease or annoy

badinage—playful talk; banter

baffle—to perplex

baleful—harmful

balk—to obstruct; to refuse to move

balm—something that soothes or heals

banal—trite; commonplace

bandy—to toss back and forth; exchange

baneful—deadly

barbaric—uncivilized

baroque—very ornate

barrage—a prolonged attack of artillery fire or words

barrister—a man of the legal profession

bastion—a fortification or defense

bate—to lessen

bathos—sentimentality

batten—to thrive

bayou—a marshy body of water

beatific—blissful

beatitude—perfect happiness

bedizen—to dress in a showy way

bedlam—a madhouse; a place of chaos

beguile—to charm or deceive

behemoth—a large and powerful animal or thing

behoof—behalf; interest

belabor—to beat; to scold or criticize

beleaguer—to besiege

belie—to contradict

bellicose—warlike

belligerent—warlike

benediction—a blessing

benefactor—one who provides benefits

benevolent—kindly

benighted—surrounded by darkness; unenlightened

benign—kindly; harmless

benison—a blessing

berate—to scold

berserk—frenzied

beset—to attack

bestial—like a beast; brutish

bestow—to present (as a gift); to confer

bestride—to mount with one leg on each side

bete noire—something or someone hated or feared

bibliophile—one who loves books

bibulous—inclined to drink alcoholic beverages

biennial—every two years

bigot—an intolerant person

bilious—bad-tempered

billingsgate—vulgar, abusive talk

binate—paired

bivouac—a temporary encampment

bizarre—odd; eccentric

blanch—to make white; to bleach; (a person) to turn white

bland—mild

blandishment—flattery

blasphemy—profanity

blatant—unpleasantly loud

blazon—to make known; to adorn or decorate

bleak—unsheltered; bare

blight—anything that kills, withers, or stunts

blithe—gay

bloated—swollen

bludgeon—a club

bluster—to act in a noisy manner

bode—to foreshadow

boisterous—rowdy

bolster—to support

bombastic—using unnecessarily pompous language

bondage—slavery

boor—a rude person

bootless—useless

bounty—generosity

bourgeois—pertaining to the middle class

bovine—cowlike

bowdlerize—to remove offensive passages (from a book)

braggadocio—a braggart

brandish—to shake or wave (something) in a menacing way

brash—impudent

bravado—a show of bravery

brazen—shameless

breach—a violation

brevity—briefness

brigand—a bandit

broach—to open or introduce

bromidic—dull

bruit—to rumor

brusque—abrupt in manner

bucolic—rural; pastoral

buffoonery—clowning

bullion—gold or silver in bars

bulwark—a defense

bumptious—conceited or forward

burgeon—to grow

burlesque—to imitate in order to ridicule

burnish—to polish

buttress—a support

buxom—healthy; plump

C

cabal—a small group of conspirators

cache—a hiding place; hidden things

cacophony—harsh sound

cadaver—a corpse

cadence—rhythm

cadre—a basic structure; a nucleus or framework

caitiff—a mean person

cajole—to coax or wheedle

caliber—quality or value

calk, caulk—to fill cracks or seams

calligraphy—penmanship

callous—unfeeling

callow—immature

calumny—slander

camaraderie—fellowship

canaille—rabble; mob

canard—a false, often malicious report

candor—frankness

canny—shrewd

cant—slang or argot

canvass—to go through for opinions, votes, etc.

capacious—roomy

capitulate—to surrender

capricious—erratic, changeable

captious—quick to find fault

captivate—to fascinate

careen—to lean to the side or from side to side

caricature—an imitation or drawing that exaggerates certain features of the subject

carmine—red

carnage—slaughter

carnal—bodily

carousal—a rowdy drinking party

carp—to make petty complaints

carrion—decaying flesh

carte blanche—a free hand; unlimited authority

castigate—to punish

casually—a mishap

casuistry—false reasoning

cataclysm—an upheaval

catalyst—an agent of change

catapult—to shoot or launch; to leap

catastrophe—a calamity

categorical—absolute

catholic—universal

causerie—a chat

caustic—corrosive

cauterize—to burn

cavalcade—a procession

caveat—a warning

cavil—to quibble

cede—to give up one's rights to (something); to transfer ownership of

celerity—speed

celestial—heavenly

celibate—unmarried

censure—to blame or criticize

cerebration—thought; thinking

cessation—stopping

cession—the giving up (of something) to another

chafe—to rub for warmth; to irritate

chaff—husks of grain; anything worthless

chagrin—embarrassment

chaotic—totally disorderly

charlatan—imposter; quack

chary—watchful

chaste—pure

chastise—to punish

chattel—personal property

chauvinism—fanatical patriotism or partisanship

checkered—characterized by diverse experiences

chicanery—trickery or deception

chide—to rebuke

chimerical—imaginary

choleric—quick-tempered

chronic—long-lasting or perpetual

chronicle—a historical record arranged in order of time

churlish—rude

circuitous—roundabout

circumlocution—an indirect or lengthy way of saying something

circumscribe—to encircle

circumspect—cautious

circumvent—to surround; to prevent (something) by cleverness

citadel—a fortress

cite—to quote

civility—politeness

clandestine—secret

clarion—clear (sound) like a trumpet

cleave—to split

cleft—a split

clemency—leniency

cliché—an overworked expression

climacteric—a crucial period or event

climactic—pertaining to the climax, or high point

clique—an exclusive group of people

cloister—a monastery or convent

cloy—to satiate

coadjutor—an assistant

coalesce—to unite or merge

codicil—an addition or supplement

coerce—to force

coffer—a strongbox

cogent—forceful

cogitate—to think over

cognate—related

cognizant—aware

cognomen—a name

cohesion—tendency to stick together

cohort—a group or band; an associate

coincident—happening at the same time

collaborate—to work together

collateral—side by side; parallel

collocation—an arrangement

colloquial—conversational; informal (speech)

colloquy—a formal discussion or conference

collusion—conspiracy

colossal—huge

comatose—pertaining to a coma

comely—attractive

comestible—edible

comity—politeness

commensurate—equal in size or measure

comminuted—powdered

commiseration—sympathy or sorrow

commodious—spacious

commutation—an exchange or substitution

compassion—deep sympathy

compatible—able to get along well together

compendious—brief but comprehensive

compile—to gather in an orderly form

complacent—self-satisfied

complaisant—obliging; agreeable

complement—that which completes something

compliant—submissive

component—a part of the whole

comport—to behave or conduct (oneself)

compunction—guilt; remorse

concatenate—linked together; connected

concede—to acknowledge or admit as true

conciliate—to make up with

concise—brief and clear

conclave—a private or secret meeting

conclusive—decisive

concoct—to devise

concomitant—accompanying

concordat—an agreement

concourse—a crowd; a space for crowds to gather

concupiscent—having strong sexual desire or lust

concurrent—running together or at the same time

condescend—to deal with someone beneath oneself on his own level, sometimes patronizingly

condign—deserved or suitable

condolence—expression of sympathy

condone—to pardon or overlook

conducive—tending or leading

conduit—a pipe or channel for liquids

configuration—an arrangement

confiscate—to seize by authority

connagration—a large fire

confute—to prove wrong

congeal—to solidify

congenital—existing from birth

conglomerate—a mass or cluster

congruent—corresponding

congruous—suitable, fitting

conjecture—a guess

conjoin—to unite

conjugal—pertaining to marriage

conjure—to produce by magic

connive—to pretend not to see another's wrongdoing; to cooperate or conspire in wrongdoing

connoisseur—one with expert knowledge and taste in an area

connotation—an idea suggested by a word or phrase that is different from the literal meaning of the word or phrase

consanguinity—blood relationship; close relationship

conscript—to draft (as for military service)

consecrate—to dedicate

consensus—general agreement

consign—to hand over; to put in the care of another

consonance—agreement

consort—a spouse, particularly of a king or queen; a traveling companion

consternation—great emotion that leaves one helpless and confused

constituency—the people served by an elected official

constrain—to confine or hold back

constrict—to make smaller by applying pressure; to restrict

construe—to interpret

consummate—to bring to completion; to finish

contaminate—to pollute

contemn—to scorn

contentious—quarrelsome; controversial

context—the words around a particular portion of a speech or passage; surroundings and background

contiguous—touching along one side; adjacent

continence—self-restraint; moderation

contingent—possible; accidenlal; depending on something else

contortion—a twisting

contraband—smuggled merchandise

contravene—to oppose; to dispute

contrition—remorse or repentance

contrivance—something that is thought up or devised; an invention

controvert—to contradict; to debate

contumacious—insubordinate; disobedient

contumely—humiliating rudeness

contusion—bruise

conundrum—a puzzling question or problem

convene—to assemble

conversant—familiar (with)

conveyance—a vehicle or other means of carrying

convivial—pertaining to festivity; sociable

convoke—to call together

convolution—a twisting together; a twist or coil

copious—plentiful

corollary—a proposition that follows from another that has been proved

corporeal—bodily

corpulent—very fat

correlation—a mutual relationship; a correspondence

corroborate—to confirm

corrosive—capable of eating or wearing away; sarcastic; biting

corsair—a pirate or pirate ship

cortege—a procession

coterie—a clique

countermand—to revoke (an order)

coup d'etat—an overthrow of a government

covenant—an agreement

covert—hidden

covetous—envious

cower—to shrink in fear

coy—bashful; reserved; coquettish

cozen—to cheat or deceive

crabbed—ill-tempered

crass—grossly stupid or dull

craven—cowardly

credence—belief

credulous—easily or too easily convinced

creed—a statement of belief, religious or otherwise

crepilate—to crackle

criterion—a standard for judging

crone—a hag

crony—a close companion

crux—a problem; the deciding point

cryptic—hidden

cudgel—a stick or club

culinary—pertaining to the kitchen or cooking

cull—to pick or select

culmination—the highest point

culpable—blameworthy

cumbersome—burdensome; clumsy

cuneate—wedge-shaped

cupidity—greed

curmudgeon—a bad-tempered person

curry—to try to obtain favor by flattery

cursory—superficial

curtail—to cut short

cynic—a person who believes all actions are motivated by selfishness

D

dais—a platform in a hall or room

dally—to play or trifle; to waste time

dank—damp

dastard—a mean coward

daunt—to intimidate

dauntless—bold

dearth—scarcity

debacle—an overwhelming defeat or failure

debase—to lower in dignity, quality, or value

debauch—to corrupt

debilitate—to weaken

debonair—courteous; gay

decadence—decay

decamp—to break camp; to run away

deciduous—falling off at a certain time or yearly (as leaves from trees)

decimate—to kill a large part of

declivity—a downgrade; a slope

decorous—proper

decoy—a lure or bait

decrepit—weak from age

decry—to speak against publicly

deduce—to reason out logically; to conclude from known facts

de facto—actual

defalcate—to misuse money left in one's care; to embezzle

defamation—slander

default—neglect; failure to do what is required

defection—desertion

deference—regard for another's wishes

defile—to make dirty or pollute; to dishonor

definitive—conclusive; distinguishing

deflect—to turn aside; to deviate

defunct—dead; no longer operating

deign—to condescend

delete—to strike out or erase

deleterious—harmful

delineate—to sketch or design; to portray

delude—to mislead

delusion—a false belief

demagogue—one who stirs people up by emotional appeal in order to gain power

demarcate—to mark the limits of

demean—to degrade

demeanor—bearing or behavior

demise—death

demolition—destruction

demonic—pertaining to a demon or demons

demur—to delay; to object

demure—serious; prim

denizen—an inhabitant

denouement—the outcome or solution of a plot

depict—to portray

depilate—to rid of hair

deplete—to reduce or exhaust

deplore—to lament or feel sorry about

deploy—to station forces or troops in a planned way

depravity—corruption

deprecate—to express disapproval of

depreciate—to lessen in value

depredate—to plunder or despoil

deranged—insane

derelict—abandoned

deride—to mock; to laugh at

derogatory—expressing a low opinion

descant—to discuss at length

descry—to detect (something distant or obscure)

desecrate—to make profane

desiccate—to dry up

desist—to stop

despicable—contemptible

despoil—to strip; to pillage

despotism—tyranny

destitute—lacking; in extreme need of things

desuetude—state of disuse

desultory—aimless; random

deterrent—something that discourages (someone) from an action

detonate—to explode

detraction—belittling the worth of something or someone

detriment—injury; hurt

deviate—to turn aside

devious—winding; going astray

devoid—lacking

devolve—to transfer to another person

devout—pious

dexterous—skillful

diabolical—devilish

diadem—a crown

diapason—the entire range of musical sounds

diaphanous—transparent or translucent

diatribe—a bitter denunciation

dichotomy—a division into two parts

dictum—an authoritative statement

didactic—instructive

diffident—unconfident; timid

diffusion—the act of spreading (something) out in all directions

digress—to turn aside or deviate, specially in writing or speaking

dilapidation—a state of disrepair

dilate—to expand

dilatory—tending to delay; tardy

dilemma—a choice of two unsatisfactory alternatives

dilettante—one who involves himself in the arts as a pastime

diligent—hard-working

diminution—a lessening

dint—means

dire—terrible; fatal; extreme

dirge—funereal music

disavowal—a denial

discernible—able to be seen or distinguished

discerning—having good judgment; astute

disclaim—to disown

discomfit—to frustrate the plans of

disconcert—to upset or confuse

disconsolate—sad; dejected

discordant—not harmonious

discountenance—to make ashamed; to discourage

discreet—showing good judgment in conduct; prudent

discrete—separate; not connected

discretion—individual judgment; quality of being discreet

discursive—passing from one subject to another

disdain—to think (someone or something) unworthy

disheveled—messy

disingenuous—insincere

disinterested—not influenced by personal advantage

disjointed—disconnected

disparage—to belittle

disparity—inequality

disperse—to scatter or distribute

disport—to amuse or divert

disputatious—inclined to dispute

disquisition—a formal inquiry; an elaborate essay

dissemble—to disguise or pretend

disseminate—to scatter

dissident—not agreeing

dissimulate—to dissemble; to pretend

dissipate—to scatter or disperse

dissolute—loose in morals

dissonance—discord

dissuade—to advise against; to divert by persuasion

distend—to expand

distrait—absent-minded; preoccupied

distraught—troubled; confused; harassed

diurnal—daily

diverge—to extend from one point in separate directions

diverse—differing; various

divest—to strip or deprive

divination—the act of foreseeing or foretelling

divulge—to reveal

docile—easy to teach or discipline

doff—to take off

doggerel—poorly written verse

dogma—a belief or doctrine; a positive statement of opinion

dogmatic—positive in manner or in what one says

doldrums—low spirits

dolorous—sorrowful

dolt—a stupid fellow

domicile—a home

dormant—sleeping; inactive

dorsal—pertaining to the back

dossier—collected docments on a person

dotage—senility

doughty—valiant

dour—stern; sullen

dregs—sediment; the most worthless part of something

drivel—silly talk

droll—amusing and strange

dross—waste or refuse

drudgery—tiresome work

dubious—doubtful

ductile—able to be drawn or hammered thin without breaking

dulcet—sweet-sounding

duplicity—deception;

double—dealing

durance—imprisonment

duress—imprisonment; compulsion

E

ebullient—enthusiastic

eccentricity—oddity

éclat—brilliant success; acclaim

eclectic—made up of material collected from many sources

ecumenical—universal; intended to bring together the Christian churches

edict—a decree

edifice—a (usually large) building

edify—to instruct and improve

educe—to elicit or draw forth

efface—to rub out

effectual—efficient

effervesce—to bubble; to be lively or boisterous

effete—exhausted; worn out

efficacy—power to have effect

elligy—an image or figure that represents a disliked person

effluence—a flowing forth

effrontery—shameless boldness

effulgent—radiant

effusive—pouring out; gushing

egotism—constant reference to oneself

egregious—flagrant

egress—emergence; exit

elation—high spirits

eleemosynary—pertaining to charity

elegy—a poem, particularly a lament for the dead

elicit—to draw out

elucidate—to explain; to throw light on

elusive—hard to grasp

emaciated—very thin

emanate—to flow forth

embellish—to ornament or beautify

embody—to give bodily form to; to make concrete

embroil—to confuse by discord; to involve in confusion

embryonic—undeveloped

emend—to correct

eminent—lofty; distinguished

emollient—something that soothes or softens (the body)

emolument—one's fees or salary

empirical—based on observation or experience

empyreal—heavenly

emulate—to imitate with the hope of equaling or surpassing

enclave—an area enclosed inside a foreign territory

encomium—high praise

encompass—to encircle; to contain

encroach—to trespass

encumber—to impede or burden

endemic—native to a particular area

endue—to invest or endow

enervate—to weaken

engender—to cause or produce

engrossed—absorbed; fully occupied

engulf—to swallow up or overwhelm

enhance—to make greater; to heighten

enigma—a puzzle

enjoin—to order; to prohibit

ennui—boredom

enormity—great wickedness

ensconce—to shelter; to settle comfortably

ensue—to follow right after

enthrall—to captivate

entity—a being or thing

entourage—a group of associates or attendants

entreaty—a serious request

entrepreneur—a man of business

envenom—to make poisonous; to embitter

environs—surroundings; vicinity

ephemeral—short-lived

epicure—a connoisseur of food and drink

epigram—a short, pointed poem or saying

epistle—a long, formal letter

epithet—a descriptive phrase; an uncomplimentary name

epitome—an abstract; a part that represents the whole

epoch—a period of time

equable—uniform; tranquil

equanimity—even temper

equestrian—pertaining to horses

equilibrium—a state of balance between various forces or factors

equity—fairness

equivocal—ambiguous; doubtful

equivocate—to deceive; to lie

erode—to eat away

errant—wandering

erudite—scholarly

escarpment—a steep slope

eschew—to avoid

esculent—edible

esoteric—for a limited, specially initiated group

espouse—to marry; to advocate (a cause)

esprit de corps—group spirit

estimable—worthy of respect or esteem

estival—pertaining to summer

estranged—separated

ethereal—celestial; spiritual

ethnic—pertaining to races or cultures

eugenic—pertaining to the bearing of genetically healthy offspring

eulogy—high praise

euphemism—an inoffensive expression substituted for an unpleasant one

euphoria—a feeling of well-being

euthanasia—painless death

evanescent—fleeting

evasive—not frank or straightforward

evince—to make evident; to display

eviscerate—to disembowel

evoke—to call forth

evolve—to develop gradually; to unfold

exacerbate—to make more intense; to aggravate

exact—to call for; to require

exasperate—to vex

excise—to cut away

excoriate—to strip of skin; to denounce harshly

exculpate—to free from blame

execrable—detestable

exemplary—serving as a good example

exhort—to urge

exigency—an emergency

exiguous—meager

exonerate—to acquit

exorbitant—excessive; extravagant

exorcise—to drive out (an evil spirit)

expatiate—to talk freely and at length

expedient—advantageous

expedite—to speed up or make easy

expeditious—efficient and quick

expiate—to atone for

expound—to set forth

expunge—to blot out; to erase

expurgate—to rid (a book) of offensive material

extant—in existence

extemporaneous—not planned

extenuate—to make thin; to diminish

extirpate—to pluck out

extol—to praise

extort—to take from a person by force

extradition—the surrender by one state to another of an alleged criminal

extraneous—not essential

extricate—to free

extrinsic—unessential; extraneous

extrovert—one whose interest is directed outside himself

extrude—to force or push out

exuberant—profuse; effusive

exude—to discharge or ooze; to radiate; to diffuse

F

fabricate—to build; to lie

façade—the front of a building

facet—a small plane of a gem; an aspect

facetious—humorous; joking

facile—easy; expert

facilitate—to make easier

faction—a clique or party

factious—producing or tending to dissension

factitious—artificial

factotum—an employee with many duties

faculty—an ability; a sense

fain—gladly

fallacious—misleading; containing a fallacy

fallible—capable of error

fallow—(land) left unplanted during a growing season

falter—to move unsteadily; to stumble or stammer

fanaticism—excessive enthusiasm

fastidious—hard to please; easy to offend

fatalism—the belief that all events are ruled by fate

fatuous—foolish

fauna—animal life

faux pas—an error in social behavior

fawn—to seek favor by demeaning oneself

fealty—loyalty

feasible—practical

feckless—weak; careless

feculent—filthy; foul

fecundity—fertility; productiveness

feign—to pretend

feint—a move intended to throw one's opponent off guard

felicitous—apt; happy in expression

fell—cruel; fierce

felonious—wicked

ferment—a state of unrest

ferret—to search out

fervent, fervid—hot; ardent

fete—a lavish entertainment, often in someone's honor

fetid—stinking

fetish—an object supposed to have magical power; any object of special devotion

felter—to shackle or restrain

fettle—state of the body and mind

fiasco—a complete failure

fiat—a command

fickle—changeable

fidelity—faithfulness

fiduciary—pertaining to one who holds something in trust for another

figment—an invention; a fiction

filch—to steal

filial—pertaining to a son or daughter

finale—a conclusion

finesse—skill; cunning

finite—limited

fissure—a narrow opening or cleft

flaccid—flabby

flag—to droop or lose vigor

flagellate—to whip or flog

flagitious—wicked and vile

flagrant—glaring (as an error)

flail—to beat

flamboyant—ornate; showy

flatulent—gas-producing; windy in speech

flaunt—to show off; to display

flay—to skin; to pillage; to censure harshly

fledgling—a young bird that has his feathers; an immature person

flippant—pert

florid—flowery; ornate

flotsam—ship wreckage floating on the sea; drifting persons or things

flout—to reject

fluctuate—to waver

fluent—fluid; easy with words

flux—a moving; a flowing

foible—a failing or weakness

foist—to pass off fraudulently

foment—to stir up

foppish—like a dandy

foray—a raid

forbearance—patience

foreboding—a feeling of coming evil

formidable—threatening

forswear—to renounce

forte—strong point

fortitude—strength; courage

fortuitous—accidental

foster—to rear; to promote

fractious—unruly

fraught—filled

fray—a commotion or fight

freebooter—a plunderer; a pirate

frenetic—frantic; frenzied

frenzy—violent emotional excitement

fresco—a painting done on fresh plaster

freshet—a stream or rush of water

frigid—very cold

fritter—to waste

frivolous—of little importance or value; trivial

froward—obstinate

fructify—to bear fruit

frugal—thrifty

fruition—use or realization; enjoyment

frustrate—to counteract; to prevent from achieving something

fulminate—to explode suddenly; to thunder forth verbally

fulsome—offensive particularly because of insincerity

funereal—appropriate to funerals

furor—a fury or frenzy

furtive—stealthy

fusion—union

futile—useless

G

gadfly—a fly that attacks livestock; a person who annoys people or moves them to action

gainsay—to deny

gambol—to skip and frolic

gamut—the whole range

gape—to open wide

gargantuan—gigantic

garish—gaudy

garner—to gather or store

garnish—to decorate

garrulous—talkative

gasconade—boastful talk

gelid—icy; frozen

generality—a broad, vague statement

generic—pertaining to a whole class, kind, or group

genial—favorable to growth; kindly

genre—a kind or category

gentility—of the upper classes; having taste and refinement

gentry—people of education and good birth

germane—relevant and pertinent to the case at hand

germinal—in the first stage of growth

gesticulation—gesture

ghastly—horrible

gibbet—gallows

gibe—to scoff at; to deride

gist—the main point in a debate or question

glaucous—bluish- or yellowish-green

glean—to gather what has been left in a field after reaping; to pick up, little by little

glib—fluent

gloaming—dusk

gloar—to look at with evil satisfaction or greed

glur—to overfill

glutinous—gluey

gluttony—excess in eating

gnarled—twisted

gnomic—wise and pithy

goad—to urge; to drive

gorge—to stuff

gouge—to scoop out; to tear out

gradation—arrangement by grades or steps

gradient—a slope; the degree of a slope

graphic—vivid; pertaining to writing

granary—a storehouse for grain

grandiloquent—using pompous language

grandiose—imposing; splendid

gratis—free

gratuitous—given freely; unwarranted

gregarious—tending to flock together

grimace—an expression that twists the face

grotesque—distorted; bizarre; absurd

grotto—a cave

grovel—to lie prone; to act humble or abject

grueling—punishing

gudgeon—a person who is easy to trick

guerdon—a reward

guile—deceit

guileless—innocent

gullible—easily tricked

gustatory—pertaining to tasting

gusto—liking; great appreciation or relish

guttural—pertaining to the throat

H

habiliments—clothing; equipment

habitable—able or fit to be lived in

hackneyed—trite

haggard—unruly; looking worn and wasted from exertion or emotion

haggle—to bargain

halcyon—peaceful

hale—healthy and sound

hallucination—a perception of something imaginary

hamper—to obstruct or hinder

haphazard—random

hapless—unlucky

harangue—a long speech; a tirade

harass—to worry or torment

harbinger—a forerunner

harp—to persist in talking or writing (about something)

harridan—a shrewish old woman

harrow—to rob or plunder

harry—to raid; to torment or worry

haughty—showing scorn for others; proud

hauteur—haughtiness

hawser—a large rope or cable for mooring or anchoring a ship

hector—to bully

hedonism—the pursuit of pleasure as the primary goal of life

heedless—careless; unmindful

hegemony—leadership; dominance

heinous—abominable

herbaceous—pertaining to herbs or leaves

herculean—of great size, strength, or courage

heresy—a religious belief opposed by the church

heterodox—unorthodox; inclining toward heresy

heterogeneous—dissimilar; varied

hiatus—a gap or break

hibernal—pertaining to winter

hierarchy—an arrangement in order of rank

hieratic—priestly

hieroglyphic—written in symbols; hard to read or understand

hilarity—mirth

hinder—to restrain or hold back

hirsute—hairy

histrionic—theatrical

hoary—white; white-haired

holocaust—destruction by fire

homage—allegiance or honor

homicide—tbe killing of one person by another

homily—a long, dull sermon

homogeneous—similar; uniform

hone—to sharpen

hortatory—encouraging; giving advice

horticulture—the growing of plants

hybrid—of mixed or unlike parts

hydrous—containing water

hyperbole—exaggeration

hypercritical—too critical

hypochondriac—one who constantly believes he is ill

hypocritical—pretending to be what one is not

hypothetical—assumed; supposed

I

iconoclast—one who attacks traditional ideas

ideology—a body of ideas

idiom—a language or dialect; a particular phrasing that is accepted in use, altbough its meaning may be different from the literal meaning of the words

idiosyncrasy—a personal peculiarity

idolatry—worship

idyll—a poem based on a simple scene

igneous—pertaining to or produced by fire

ignoble—dishonorable; base

ignominious—shameful; degrading

illicit—unlawful; prohibited

illusory—unreal; deceptive

imbibe—to drink. drink in, or absorb

imbroglio—a confusion; a misunderstanding

imbue—to color; to inspire (with ideas)

immaculate—spotless; clean

immanent—existing within

imminent—ahout to happen

immolate—to sacrifice

immutable—unchangeable

impair—to make worse or weaker; to reduce

impale—to fix on a pointed object

impalpable—not capable of being felt; not capable of being grasped by the mind

impasse—a situation with no escape or solution

impassive—not feeling pain; calm

impeccable—faultless

impecunious—poor; penniless

impede—to obstruct or delay

impending—about to happen

impenitent—without regret

imperious—domineering

impermeable—unable to be penetrated

impertinent—irrelevant; impudent

imperturbable—unable to be disturbed; impassive

impervious—impenetrable; not affected (by something)

impetuous—rushing; rash or impulsive

impetus—a force; a driving force

impiety—lack of reverence (for God or parents)

implacable—incapable of being pacified

implicate—to involve; to imply

implicit—implied: absolute

impolitic—unwise

import—meaning; significance

importune—to urge persistently

impotent—weak; powerless

imprecate—to pray for (evil)

impregnable—unable to be conquered or entered

impresario—a manager in the performing arts

impromptu—offhand

impropriety—being improper

improvident—not providing for the future

impugn—to oppose or challenge

impunity—freedom from punishment or harm

impute—to charge another (with a negative trait)

inadvertent—heedless; unintentional

inane—empty; foolish

inarticulate—unable to speak understandably or at all

incantation—a chant supposed to work magic

incapacitate—to disable

incarcerate—to imprison

incendiary—pertaining to destruction by fire

inception—beginning

incessant—never-ending

inchoate—just begun; incipient

incipient—in the first stage of existence

incisive—keen, sharp

inclement—stormy; harsh

incognito—disguised

incongruous—incompatible; inappropriate

inconsequential—unimportant

incontrovertible—undeniable

incorrigible—unreformable

increment—increase; the amount of increase

incriminate—to accuse of a crime; to involve in a crime

incubus—a nightmare; an oppressive burden

inculcate—to instill

inculpate—to incriminate

incursion—an inroad; a brief raid

indefatigable—untiring

indemnify—to insure; to reimburse

indict—to charge formally with

indigenous—growing or living in a particular area

indite—to compose and write

indolent—lazy; idle

indomitable—hard to discourage or defeat

indubitable—unquestionable

indulgent—giving in to one's own desires; kind or lenient

indurate—hardened

ineffable—inexpressible

ineluctable—unavoidable

inept—unfit; clumsy

inert—powerless to move; slow

inexorable—unrelenting; unalterable

infallible—incapable of error

infamous—notorious

inference—something that is drawn as a conclusion

infernal—pertaining to hell; diabolical

infidel—one who doesn't believe in a particular doctrine or religion

infinite—limitless; vast

infirmity—weakness

influx—a flowing in

infringe—to violate

ingenious—having genius; clever; original

ingenuous—candid; frank

ingrate—an ungrateful person

ingratiate—to win another's favor by efforts

inherent—innate; characteristic

inhibit—to hold back or repress

inimical—hostile; in opposition

iniquitous—wicked

injunction—a command; an order enjoining, or prohibiting, (someone) from doing something

innate—existing in someone from birth or in something by its nature

innocuous—harmless; noncontroversial

innuendo—an indirect remark or reference

inordinate—unregulated; immoderate

inscrutable—obscure; not easily understood

insensate—not feeling; inanimate; insensitive

insidious—crafty

insinuate—to work gradually into a state; to hint

insipid—tasteless; dull

insolent—impudent; disrespectful

insolvent—bankrupt; unable to pay debts

insouciant—carefree; indifferent

instigate—to urge on to some action; to incite

insular—like an island; isolated; narrowminded

insuperable—unable to be overcome

insurgent—a person who rises up against (political) authority

intangible—unable to be touched; impalpable

integrity—wholeness; soundness; honesty

intelligentsia—intellectuals as a group

inter—to bury

interdict—to prohibit; to restrain or impede

interim—meantime

interjection—something thrown in or interrupted with; an exclamation

intermittent—periodic; starting and stopping

internecine—mutually harmful or destructive

interpolate—to insert

interregnum—a break, as between governments or regimes

intestate—without a (legal) will to distribute one's property after death

intimate—to hint

intractable—unruly or stubborn

intransigent—refusing to agree or compromise

intrepid—fearless

intrinsic—inherent; of the nature of a thing

introvert—a person who looks inside himself more than outside

intuition—immediate understanding

inundate—to flood

inured—habituated (to something unpleasant)

invective—a violent verbal attack

inveigh—to talk or write strongly (against)

inveigle—to trick or entice

inverse—opposite

investiture—the giving of office to someone

inveterate—of long standing

invidious—offensive

inviolable—not to be violated; unable to be violated

invulnerable—unable to be injured or wounded

iota—a tiny amount

irascible—quick-tempered

irksome—tiresome; annoying

irony—humor in which one says the opposite of what he means; an occurrence that is the opposite of what is expected

irremediable—incurable or irreparable

irrevocable—unable to be called back or undone

iterate—to repeat

itinerant—traveling

J

jaded—tired; satiated

jargon—incoherent speech; a mixed language; the particular vocabulary of one group

jaundiced—yellow; prejudiced

jeopardy—peril

jettison—to throw overboard

jetty—a wall built out into the water

jocose—humorous

jocular—joking

jocund—cheerful

journeyman—a worker who has learned a trade

judicious—wise

juggernaut—any extremely strong and irresistible force

juncture—a point of joining; a critical point in the development of events

junket—a feast or picnic; a pleasure excursion

junta—men engaged in political intrigue

juxtapose—to place side by side

K

ken—understanding

kinetic—pertaining to motion

kith—friends

knavery—dishonesty; deceit

knell—to ring solemnly

knoll—a small hill

L

labyrinth—a maze

lacerate—to tear or mangle

lachrymose—tearful

lackadaisical—spiritless; listless

laconic—brief; using few words

lacuna—a gap where something is missing

laggard—one who is slow

laity—all the people who are not clergy

lambent—flickering; glowing

lampoon—to attack or ridicule

languid—weak; listless

languish—to lose vigor; to droop

larceny—theft

largess—generosity

lascivious—lewd; lustful

lassitude—weariness

latent—hidden or undeveloped

lateral—pertaining to the side or sides

latitude—freedom to act

laudatory—praising

leaven—to spread something throughout something else to bring about a gradual change

lecherous—lustful

legerdemain—trickery

lesion—an injury

lethal—deadly

lethargic—dull; sluggish

levity—gaiety

liaison—a linking up

libel—false printed material intended to harm a person's reputation

libertine—one who lives a morally unrestrained life

libidinous—lustful; lewd

licentious—morally unrestrained

liege—a name for a feudal lord or his subject

lieu—place (in lieu of)

limn—to paint or draw; to describe in words

limpid—clear

literal—word-for-word; actual

lithe—flexible; limber

litigation—carrying out a lawsuit

littoral—pertaining to the shore or coast

livid—black-and-blue; lead-colored

loath—reluctant

loathe—to detest

locution—a word or phrase; a style of speech

logistics—the part of military science having to do with obtaining and moving men and material

longevity—long life

loquacious—talkative

lout—a stupid person

lubricity—smoothness; trickiness

lucent—shining; giving off light

lucid—transparent; clear

lucrative—profitable

lucre—money

ludicrous—absurd

lugubrious—mournful

luminary—a body that sheds light; a person who enlightens; any famous person

lurid—sensational

lustrous—shining

luxuriant—lush; rich

M

macabre—gruesome; horrible

macerate—to soften by soaking; to break or tear into small pieces

Machiavellian—crafty and deceitful

machination—a secret plot or scheme

magnanimous—generous; not petty

magnate—an important person, often in a business

magniloquent—lofty or pompous

maim—to disable or mutilate (a person)

maladroit—clumsy

malaise—a vague feeling of illness

malcontent—discontented

malediction—a curse

malefactor—one who does evil

malevolent—wishing ill to others

malfeasance—a wrongdoing

malicious—spiteful

malign—to slander

malignant—evil; harmful

malinger—to pretend to be ill to avoid doing something

malleable—able to be hammered; pliable

mammoth—enormous

mandate—an official order or command

mandatory—required

maniacal—insane; raving

manifest—apparent or evident

manipulate—to work with the hands; to control by unfair means

manumission—liberation from slavery

marauder—a raider

maritime—pertaining to the sea

martial—pertaining to war or the military; warlike

martinet—a strict disciplinarian

masochist—one who enjoys suffering

masticate—to chew up

maternal—pertaining to a mother or motherhood

matrix—a die or mold

maudlin—foolishly sentimental

maunder—to act dreamily or vaguely

mauve—purple

maverick—one who refuses to go along with his group

mawkish—sickeningly sweet

maxim—a principle or truth precisely stated; a saying

mayhem—maiming another person; violence or destruction

meander—to wind or wander

mecca—a place where many people visit

mediate—to help two opposing sides come to agreement

mediocre—ordinary; average

mélange—a mixture

melee—a noisy fight among a lot of people

meliorate—to improve

mellifluous—sweet and smooth

mendacious—lying

mendicant—a beggar

menial—pertaining to servants; servile

mentor—a wise advisor or teacher

mercantile—pertaining to merchants or trade

mercenary—motivated by money; greedy

mercurial—like mercury; quick; changeable

meretricious—superficially alluring

mesa—a high, flat land with steep sides

metamorphosis—a change or transformation

metaphysical—pertaining to the nature of being or reality

mete—to distribute

meticulous—very careful about details

mettle—quality of character, especially good character

miasma—a vapor rising from a swamp; an unwholesome atmosphere

mien—manner or bearing

migrant—a person or an animal that moves from place to place

militate—to work (against)

mimetic—imitative

mimic—to imitate

minatory—threatening

mincing—acting overly dainty or elegant

minion—a favorite (follower); a subordinate

ministration—the carrying out of a minister's duties; service

minutiae—minor details

misadventure—a bit of bad luck

misanthrope—one who dislikes other people

misapprehension—misunder-standing

miscegenation—marriage between a man and a woman of different races

miscellany—a collection of varied things

misconstrue—to misinterpret

miscreant—an evil person

misdemeanor—a minor offense

misgiving—a doubt or fear

mishap—an unfortunate accident

misnomer—the wrong name applied to something

misogynist—one who hates women

mitigate—to make less painful

mnemonic—helping the memory

mobile—capable of moving or being moved

mode—a manner or style

modicum—a bit

modish—in style

modulate—to adjust or regulate

moiety—a share

mollify—to pacify

molt—to shed skin or other outer parts

molten—melted

momentous—very important

monetary—pertaining to money

monolith—a large piece of stone

moot—debatable

morbid—pertaining to disease; gruesome

mordant—biting; sarcastic

mores—ways or customs that are quite important to a culture

moribund—dying

morose—gloomy

mortify—to punish (oneself) by self-denial; to make (someone) feel ashamed

mote—a speck

motif—a main feature or theme

motility—ability to move by itself

motley—of many colors; made up of many unlike parts

mountebank—a quack

mufti—civilian clothes

mulet—to fine; to get money from someone by deceit

multiplicity—a great number (of various things)

mundane—worldly; commonplace

munificent—generous; lavish

muse—to ponder

mutable—changeable

mute—silent

mutilate—to damage by cutting off or injuring vital parts

mutinous—inclined to rebel or revolt

myopia—nearsightedness

myriad—a great number

N

nadir—the lowest point

naiad—a water nymph; a female swimmer

naiveté—simplicity; lack of sophistication

narcissism—love for and interest in the self

nascent—being born; starting to develop

natal—pertaining to one's birth

nauseous—sickening

nebulous—vague; indefinite

necromancy—black magic

nefarious—wicked

negation—denial; the absence of a positive quality

negligible—so unimportant that it can be neglected

nemesis—fair punishment; something that seems to defeat a person constantly

neolithic—pertaining to the Stone Age

neophyte—a beginner

nepotism—special consideration to relatives, particularly in assignment to offices or positions

nettle—to sting; to irritate or annoy

neurosis—a mental disorder

nexus—a connection

nicety—exactness and delicacy

niggardly—stingy

nihilist—one who believes there is no basis for knowledge; one who rejects common religious beliefs

nocturnal—pertaining to night

noisome—harmful; offensive

nomadic—moving from place to place

nomenclature—a system for naming

nominal—pertaining to names; slight

nonchalant—cool; indifferent

noncommittal—not aligning oneself with any side or point of view

nondescript—having few distinguishing qualities; hard to classify

nonentity—something that exists only in the mind; something or someone of little importance

nonpareil—without equal

nonplus—to perplex

non sequitur—something that does not follow logically from what went before

nostalgia—homesickness

notorious—well-known (often unfavorably)

novice—a beginner

noxious—harmful; unwholesome

nuance—a slight variation of color, tone, etc.

nugatory—worthless

nullify—to make invalid or useless

nurture—to feed and/or raise (a child)

nutrient—a food

O

oaf—a clumsy, stupid person

obdurate—hardhearted; hardened; inflexible

obeisance—a motion of reverence

obese—very fat

obfuscate—to make unclear; to confuse

objurgate—to rebuke

oblation—an offering

oblique—slanting; indirect

obliquity—the state of being oblique

obliterate—to wipe out

oblivion—forgetfulness

obloquy—verbal abuse or the disgrace that results from it

obnoxious—offensive

obscure—dim; unclear

obsequious—too servile or submissive

obsession—an idea that persists in the mind

obsolete—out-of-date; no longer used

obstreperous—unruly

obtrude—to push out

obtrusive—pushy in calling attention to oneself

obtuse—blunt; dull

obviate—to·make unnecessary

occlude—to close; to shut in or out

occult—hidden; secret; mysterious

odious—offensive

odoriferous—having a (pleasant) odor

odyssey—a long journey

officious—providing help that is not wanted

ogle—to look at openly and with desire

oleaginous—oily

olfactory—pertaining to the sense of smell

oligarchy—a slate ruled by a few persons

ominous—threatening

omnipotent—all-powerful

omniscient—all-knowing

omnivorous—eating both animals and vegetables

onerous—burdensome

onslaught—an attack

opaque—letting no light through

opiate—a medicine or anything else that quiets and deadens

opportune—at the right time

opprobrium—disgrace

optimum—best

opulence—wealth; abundance

oracular—wise; prophetic

ordure—filth

orifice—a mouth or opening

ornate—heavily decorated; showy

ornithologist—one who studies birds

orthodox—holding the accepted beliefs of a particular group

oscillate—to move back and forth

osculate—to kiss

ossify—to harden into bone; to settle into a habit

ostensible—apparent

ostentatious—showy; pretentious

ostracize—to banish or exclude

overt—open; observable

overweening—extremely proud

P

pacifist—one who opposes war

paean—a song of joy or praise

palatable—suitable for eating

palatial—like a palace

palaver—idle talk

pall—to become boring or otherwise bothersome

palliate—to lessen or ease (pain); to excuse

pallid—pale

palpable—able to be felt or to be grasped by the senses

paltry—insignificant

panacea—a cure-all

pander—to cater to another's unworthy desires, especially sexual

panegyric—a formal tribute

panoply—a suit of armor; a protective or showy covering

paradigm—an example or model

paradox—a statement that appears false but may be true; a statement that contradicts itself and is false

paragon—a model of perfection

paramount—chief; dominant

paranoia—a state in which one believes that others are against him or that he is a great or famous person

paraphernalia—personal possessions; equipment or gear

parasite—one who lives off another without giving anything in return

paregoric—a medicine

pariah—an outcast

parity—equality

parlance—a manner of speaking or writing

paroxysm—an attack or convulsion

parricide—the killing of a parent

parry—to ward off (a blow); to evade

parsimony—stinginess

partiality—bias; prejudice

parvenu—one who has risen in wealth or power quickly

passive—yielding; nonresisting

pastoral—pertaining to shepherds or rural life in general

patent—obvious

pathetic—pitiful

pathos—a feeling of pity or sorrow

patriarch—a father and ruler

patricide—the killing of one's father

patrimony—an inheritance

paucity—scarcity

pecadillo—a minor fault

peculate—to embezzle

pecuniary—pertaining to money

pedagogue—a teacher, often a narrow-minded one

pedantic—narrow-minded in teaching

pedestrian—ordinary and uninteresting

pejorative—derogatory

pellucid—clear; easy to understand

penance—voluntary self-punishment

penchant—a taste or liking

pendant—something that hangs

pendent—hanging

penitent—sorry or ashamed

pensive—thoughtful

penurious—stingy; poverty-stricken

penury—poverty

percussion—the impact of one thing against another

perdition—damnation; hell

peregrinations—travels

peremptory—final; undeniable or unopposable; dictatorial

perennial—lasting all through the year; lasting a long time

perfidious—treacherous

perforce—necessarily

perfunctory—without care; superficial

perigee—the point nearest the earth in an orbit

peripatetic—moving or walking about

periphery—the boundary of something; the perimeter

perjury—telling a lie under oath

permeable—able to be passed through

permeate—to pass through; to spread through

permutation—a complete change

pernicious—deadly

perpetrate—to do (something bad)

perpetual—eternal

perquisite—a benefit in addition to one's regular pay; prerogative

persiflage—a light style of talking; banter

perspective—the appearance of things caused by their positions and distances; a way of seeing things in their true relation to each other

perspicacious—keen; acute in judgment

pertinacious—persistent

pertinent—relevant

perturb—to upset or alarm

peruse—to study; to read casually

pervade—to spread throughout

perverse—wrong or corrupt; perverted; stubborn

perversion—an abnormal form; a twisting or distortion

pervious—able to be passed through or penetrated; open-minded

pessimist—one who looks on the dark side and expects the worst

pestilence—an epidemic; anything harmful

petrify—to turn to stone; to harden; to stun with fear

petulant—pert; irritable

phalanx—military ranks in close formation; a group of individuals

philander—to carry on light love affairs

philanthropist—one who gives money to help others

philistine—a narrow and conventional person who ignores the arts and culture

phlegmatic—sluggish; calm

phobia—an irrational, unwarranted fear (of something)

physiognomy—one's face and facial expressions

pied—spotted

piety—truthfulness to religious duties; devotion to family

pillage—to loot or plunder

pinion—to cut or tie a bird's wings to keep it from flying; to bind a man's arms; to shackle

pious—devout

piquant—sharp or biting to the taste; stimulating

pique—to offend or provoke

pithy—meaningful; concise

pittance—a meager amount

placate—to pacify

placid—calm; quiet

plaintive—mournful

plait—to pleat or braid

platitude—a dull or commonplace remark

platonic—intellectual or spiritual but not sexual (relationship)

plaudit—applause; an expression of approval

plausible—apparently true

plebeian—a common man

plebiscite—a vote by the people on a political issue

plenary—full; complete

plenipotentiary—a man who has full power as a governmental representative

plethora—excess

plutocracy—government by the wealthy

poach—to trespass; to steal

pogrom—a systematic persecution or killing of a group

poignant—sharply affecting the senses or feelings

politic—prudent; crafty

poltroon—a coward

polygamy—having more than one husband or wife

polyglot—speaking or writing several languages

pommel—the knob on the end of a sword or on a saddle

pompous—stately; self-important

ponder—to consider carefully

portend—to foreshadow

portent—an omen

portly—stout

posit—to place in position; to set forth as fact

posterity—all future generations

posthumous—born after one's father is dead; published after the writer's death; happening after death

postprandial—after dinner

potable—drinkable

potentate—a ruler

potential—possible; latent

potpourri—a collection of varied things

poultice—a hot, soft mass, sometimes put on sore parts of the body

practicable—feasible; usable

pragmatic—practical; dealing with daily matters

prate—to chatter

precarious—uncertain; risky

precedent—a legal occurrence that is an example for future ones

precept—a rule of conduct

precipitate—to throw downward, to bring on

precipitous—like a precipice; abrupt

preclude—to make impossible; to prevent

precocious—developing earlier than usual

precursor—a forerunner

predatory—living by robbing or exploiting others; feeding on other animals

predicate—to state as a quality of someone or something; to affirm

predilection—a preference

predispose—to make receptive

preeminent—better than others in a particular quality

prefatory—introductory

prelude—opening

premeditate—to think out ahead of time

premise—a statement on which an argument is based

premonition—a forewarning; a forehoding

preponderate—to sink downward; to predominate

preposterous—absurd

prerogative—a right or privilege

presage—to warn; to predict

prescience—foreknowledge

presentiment—a premonition or foreboding

presumption—taking something upon oneself without permission; forwardness

pretentious—claiming greatness; showing off

preternatural—abnormal; supernatural

prevaricate—to avoid the truth; to lie

primordial—existing from the beginning; original

pristine—in original condition; pure and unspoiled

privy (to)—told about (something) in secret

probity—honesty

proboscis—a long snout; a nose

proclivity—a slope; a tendency

procrastinate—to delay or postpone

prodigal—wasteful; generous

prodigious—wonderful; huge

profane—nonreligious; irreverent

proffer—to offer

proficient—skilled

profligate—immoral; wasteful

profound—very deep

profusion—a great abundance

progenitor—a forefather

progeny—children or descendants

prognosis—a forecast

proletarian—a worker

prolific—producing a lot (of children, fruit, or ideas)

prolix—wordy; long-winded

promiscuous—containing many various elements; engaging in indiscriminate sexual affairs

promontory—a headland

promulgate—to make known

prone—lying face downward; disposed (to do something)

propagate—to breed or reproduce

propensity—a natural tendency

propinquity—nearness; kinship

propitiate—to appease

propitious—gracious; boding well; advantageous

proponent—one who puts forth an idea

propound—to propose

propriety—suitability

prosaic—commonplace

proscribe—to outlaw or forbid

prosody—the study or the art of verse or versification

prostrate—lying face downward; overcome

protégé—one who is helped in his career by another

protocol—a document outlining points of agreement; a system of proper conduct in diplomatic encounters

prototype—a model

protract—to prolong

protrude—to stick out

protuberant—sticking out

provident—providing for future needs

proviso—a condition (that one must meet)

provoke—to excite; to anger

prowess—boldness; skill

proximity—nearness

proxy—a person who acts for another

prudent—careful; wise

puerile—childish

pugnacious—quarrelsome

puissant—powerful

pulchritude—beauty

pulmonary—pertaining to the lungs

punctilious—careful about detail; exact

pungent—sharp: biting

punitive—pertaining to punishment

purloin—to steal

purport—to claim

purveyor—one who supplies

purview—scope; range

pusillanimous—timid; uncourageous

putative—reputed

putrid—rotten; stinking

Q

quack—one who practices medicine without training; a charlatan

quaff—to drink

quagmire—a bog; a difficult situation

quail—to lose courage

qualm—a sudden ill feeling; a sudden misgiving

quandary—a dilemma

queasy—nauseous; uneasy

quell—to subdue; to quiet

querulous—complaining

query—a question

quibble—to object to something for petty reasons

quiescent—inactive

quietude—quiet; rest

quintessence—the most perfect example

quip—a witty remark

quirk—a twist (as of luck); an evasion; a peculiarity

quixotic—like Don Quixote; romantic and idealistic

quizzical—comical; teasing; questioning

R

rabble—a mob; the masses

rabid—violent; fanatical

raillery—satire; teasing

raiment—clothing

ramification—a branching; a consequence or result of something

rampant—growing or spreading richly; wild and uncontrollable in behavior

rancid—spoiled, as stale fat

rancor—hate

rankle—to provoke anger or rancor

rant—to rave

rapacious—greedy; predatory

rapine—taking away people's property by force; plunder

rapprochement—a bringing together

rarefied—thin; refined

ratiocination—reasoning

rationalize—to explain rationally; to find motives for one's behavior that are not the true ones

raucous—loud and rowdy

ravage—to ruin

ravening—look greedily for prey

ravenous—extremely hungry

rebate—to return (part of money paid); to deduct (from a bill)

rebuke—to scold sharply

recalcitrant—stubborn; hard to handle

recant—to take back (a belief or statement)

recapitulate—to summarize

recidivist—one who falls back into crime or other bad behavior

reciprocal—done in return; occurring on both sides

recision—the act of rescinding

recluse—one who lives apart from others

reconcile—to bring together again; to make consistent

recondite—not understandable by most people; obscure

reconnaissance—looking over a situation to get information

recourse—turning to (someone or something) for help

recreant—cowardly; disloyal

recrimination—answering an attack by attacking in return

rectify—to make right

rectitude—moral uprightness

recumbent—lying down; resting

recurrent—happening again one or more times

redeem—to get back; to save from sin; to make (oneself) worthy again by making amends

redolent—sweet-smelling

redoubtable—fearful

redress—to rectify

redundant—more than enough; wordy

refection—refreshment

refraction—the bending of a light ray or sound wave

refractory—stubborn

refulgent—shining

refutation—disproof

regale—to entertain with a feast

regeneration—renewal; rebirth

regime—a system or period of government

regimen—a system of diet and other physical care designed to aid health

regressive—going backward

reimburse—to pay back

reiterate—to repeat over and over

rejuvenate—to make seem young again

relegate—to send away (to someplace)

relevant—pertaining to the matter in question

relinquish—to give (something) up

relish—to enjoy

remediable—curable; correctable

reminisce—to remember

remiss—careless in one's duty

remission—forgiveness; a letting up

remnant—remainder

remonstrate—to protest

remunerative—profitable

render—to give over; to give up; to cause to become

renegade—one who gives up his religion or cause and joins the opposition

renounce—to give up (a right, for example)

renovate—to renew

reparable—able to be repaired

reparation—a repairing; making up for a wrong

repartee—a clever reply; clever conversation back and forth

repast—a meal

repercussion—an effect of an event

repertoire—the selection of works a performer or group is prepared to perform

replenish—to refill

replete—full; stuffed

repository—a place where things are kept

reprehensible—deserving criticism

reprieve—a postponement of punishment

reprimand—a formal rebuke

reprisal—force used in retaliation for an act by another country

reproach—to make (someone) feel ashamed

reprobate—a person of no principles

reprove—to rebuke or disapprove

repudiate—to disown; to deny

repugnant—contradictory; offensive

requiem—a Mass or music for the dead

requisite—required

requite—to return or repay

rescind—to repeal (an order)

resilient—elastic; buoyant

respite—a delay; a letup

resplendent—splendid

restitution—restoration; reimbursement

restive—balky; unruly; restless

resurgent—rising again

resuscitate—to revive

retaliate—to return injury or evil in kind

retentive—holding; able to remember

reticent—speaking very little

retinue—a group of followers or attendants

retort—to answer in kind; to reply sharply or cleverly

retract—to take back

retribution—just punishment or reward

retrieve—to recover (something); to save

retroactive—applying to the past

retrograde—going backward

retrospective—looking backward

revelry—merrymaking

reverberate—to echo

reverie—a daydream

revert—to go back to a former state

revile—to abuse; to scold

revoke—to withdraw; to rescind

revulsion—a sudden change in feeling; disgust

rheumy—watery

ribald—vulgar; coarse

rife—occurring everywhere; plentiful

rigor—strictness; exactness

risible—laughable

risqué—daring

robust—healthy and strong

rococo—an elaborate architectural style

roseate—rosy; cheerful

rote—routine

rotund—rounded; stout

rubicund—reddish

rudiment—a basic principle; a first stage

rueful—pitiable; mournful

ruminate—to ponder

rummage—to search through

ruse—a trick

ruthless—cruel

S

sable—black

saccharine—pertaining to sugar; too sweet

sacerdotal—priestly

sacrilegious—in violation of something sacred

sacrosanct—holy; not to be violated

sadist—one who gets pleasure from hurting others

sagacious—perceptive; shrewd

sage—wise

salacious—lecherous; pornographic

salient—leaping; standing out; prominent

saline—salty

sallow—having a sickly, yellowish coloring

salubrious—healthful

salutary—conducive to good health

sanctity—holiness

sang-froid—coolness; calmness

sanguine—blood-colored; cheerful and optimistic

sapient—wise

sardonic—sarcastic

sartorial—pertaining to tailors or clothing

sate—to safisfy completely

satiate—to glut

saturate—to soak

saturnine—gloomy

savant—a scholar

savoir faire—tact

savor—to season; to taste or smell appreciatively

scabrous—scaly; improper

scapegoat—one who is blamed for the wrongs of another

scathing—harsh; biting

schism—a split

scintilla—a tiny bit

scintillate—to sparkle; to show verbal brilliance

scion—an offspring

scoff—to jeer (at)

scourge—a whip; a punishment

scruple—a qualm or doubt

scrupulous—very careful in doing what is correct

scrutiny—close inspection

scurrilous—coarse; vulgar

scuttle—to scurry; to sink (a ship); to abandon (a plan)

sebaceous—pertaining to fat

secede—to withdraw

secular—worldly

sedate—calm; serious

sedentary—sitting much of the time

seditious—pertaining to revolt against the government

sedulous—diligent

seethe—to boil; to foam

seine—a fishing net

seismic—pertaining to earthquakes

semantic—pertaining to meaning

semblance—appearance

senile—showing mental deterioration due to old age

sensual—pertaining to the body or the senses

sententious—pointed; full of trite wordings

sentient—feeling; conscious

sepulcher—a tomb

sequester—to set apart; to withdraw

serene—calm

serrated—having notches along the edge

servile—slavelike

sever—to separate; to cut in two

shackle—to hold back; to restrain

shambles—a slaughterhouse; a place of disorder

shard—a broken piece (of pottery)

sheathe—to put (a knife or sword) into its covering

shibboleth—a phrase or a practice that is observed by a particular group

shoddy—cheap; poorly made

shunt—to turn aside

sidereal—pertaining to the stars or constellations

simian—pertaining to monkeys

simile—a figure of speech that compares things by using like or as

simper—to smile in a silly way

simulate—to pretend or fake

sinecure—a job that requires little work

sinister—threatening; evil

sinuous—winding; devious

skeptical—doubting

skittish—playful; jumpy

skulk—to slink

slake—to satisfy

slatternly—dirty; untidy

sleazy—flimsy (as a fabric); cheap or shoddy

slothful—lazy

slough—to shed; a swamp

slovenly—careless or untidy

sluggard—a lazy person

sobriety—soberness

sojourn—a temporary stay

solecism—a misuse of grammar; a breach of manners

solicitous—expressing care; eager

soliloquy—a talking to oneself

solstice—the point at which the sun is farthest north or south of the equator

solvent—able to pay one's debts

somatic—pertaining to the body

somnambulism—sleep-walking

somnolent—sleepy; making one sleepy

sonorous—rich and full (sound)

soothsayer—one who predicts the future

sophisticated—urbane; not naive

sordid—dirty; ignoble

soupçon—a trace or hint

spasmodic—intermittent

specious—appearing correct but not really so

specter—a ghost

spectral—ghostly

splenetic—bad-tempered

spontaneous—arising naturally or by its own force

sporadic—occasional

sportive—playful

spurious—false; not real

squalid—filthy; sordid

squander—to waste

staid—sober

stalwart—sturdy; brave; firm

stamina—endurance

stark—prominent; barren; blunt

status—position or state

staunch, stanch—to stop (blood) flowing from a wound; to stop or check

stellar—pertaining to the stars

stentorian—very loud

stigma—a sign of disgrace

stilted—elevated; pompous

stint—to hold back in distributing or using

stipend—a salary or allowance

stoical—showing no reaction to various emotions or events

stolid—unexcitable

strait—a narrow waterway; a difficult situation

stratagem—a scheme or trick

striated—striped or furrowed

stricture—censure; a limitation

strident—having a harsh or shrill sound

stringent—strict

stultify—to make stupid, dull, or worthless

suave—urbane; polished

subaltern—a subordinate

subjugate—to conquer

sublimate—to purify

sublime—exalted; grand

suborn—to get someone to do something illegal

sub rosa—in private

subsequent—coming later

subservient—servile

subsidiary—supplementary; secondary

subsidy—a grant of money

subsistence—a means of providing one's basic needs

substantiate—to confirm

subterfuge—any means by which one conceals his intentions

subtle—thin; characterized by slight differences and qualities; not obvious

subversive—inclined to overthrow or harm the government

succinct—clear and brief

succor—to aid

succulent—juicy

suffuse—to spread throughout

sully—to soil

sultry—hot and close

summation—adding up

sumptuous—lavish

sunder—to split apart

sundry—miscellaneous

superannuated—too old to be of use; outdated

supercilious—haughty

superficial—pertaining to the surface aspects of something

superfluous—more than the amount needed

superlative—of the best kind; supreme

supersede—to take the place of

supine—lying on the back

supple—flexible

supplicant—one who prays for or asks for (something)

surcease—an end

surfeit—to provide too much of something; to satiate

surly—rude and ill-tempered

surmise—a guess made on the basis of little evidence

surreptitious—secret

surrogate—a substitute

surveillance—a watch over someone

sustenance—maintenance

sybaritic—loving luxury

sycophant—one who flatters to gain favor of important people

sylvan—pertaining to the woods

symmetry—balance

symposium—a meeting for the exchange of ideas

synchronize—to regulate several things so they will correspond in time

synopsis—a summary

synthesis—a putting together

synthetic—not natural; artificial

T

tacit—unspoken; understood rather than declared

taciturn—reluctant to speak

tactful—saying and doing the appropriate thing when people's feelings are involved

tactile—pertaining to the sense of touch

taint—to infect or spoil

talisman—a charm supposed to have magic power

tangible—touchable; objective

tantamount—equal (to)

tantalize—to tempt (someone) with something he cannot have

tautological—employing needless repetition of an idea

tawdry—cheap and gaudy

tawny—tan in color

tedious—tiresome

temerity—foolish boldness

temperate—moderate

template—a pattern

temporal—temporary; worldly

tenacious—holding fast

tenet—a principle

tentative—proposed but not final; hesitant

tenuous—thin; slight

tenure—the period of time for which something is held; a permanent status in a job based on length of service

tepid—lukewarm

termagant—a shrewish old woman

terminal—pertaining to the end

terrestrial—earthly; pertaining to land

terse—concise

tertiary—third

testy—irritable

theocracy—rule of a state by God or by God's authority

therapeutic—curing

thermal—pertaining to heat

thespian—pertaining to drama; an actor

thralldom—slavery

throes—pangs

thwart—to obstruct or prevent

tirade—a lengthy, violent speech

titanic—huge

tithe—a tenth of something

titular—pertaining to a title; in name only

toady—one who tries to gain another's favor; sycophant

tome—a hook, especially a large one

torpid—dormant; slow-moving

tortuous—twisting; devious

toxic—poisonous

tract—a stretch of land

tractable—easy to manage or control

traduce—to slander

trammel—to confine or entangle

tranquil—calm; peaceful

transcend—to go beyond

transcribe—to write out in one form from another

transgression—a breaking of a rule; a violation of a limit

transient—not permanent

transition—a change from one thing to another

transitory—fleeting

translucent—allowing light through

transmute—to change from one form to another

transpire—to become known

transverse—lying across

trappings—one's clothes and equipment

trauma—a severe injury or shock

travail—hard work; pain

traverse—to go across

travesty—a burlesque; a distortion (of something)

treatise—a formal, written presentation of a subject

trek—to travel slowly

tremor—a trembling; a vibration

tremulous—trembling; afraid

trenchant—keen; forceful

trepidation—uncertainty and anxiety

tribulation—great unhappiness; a trying circumstance

tribunal—a law court

trite—overworked; no longer novel

troth—truth; one's word, as a promise

truckle—to submit and be servile

truculent—cruel; rude

truism—a statement that is known to be true

trumpery—something pretentious but not worth anything

truncate—to cut off part of

truncheon—a club

tryst—a meeting

tumid—swollen; inflated

turbid—muddy; dense

turbulence—a state of commotion or agitation

turgid—swollen; pompous

turncoat—a renegade; a traitor

turnkey—a jailer

turpitude—vileness

tutelage—care; guardianship

tyro—a beginner

U

ubiquitous—omnipresent

ulterior—on the far side; later; beyond what is said

ultimate—the farthest, final, or highest

ultimatum—a nonnegotiable demand

umbrage—offense

unadulterated—pure

unanimity—agreement

unassuming—modest

unbridled—uncontrolled; free

uncanny—strange; weird

unconscionable—done without applying one's conscience

uncouth—clumsy; not having culture or polish

unction—ointment; an intense manner of behavior; unctuousness

unctuous—oily; displaying fake religious feeling

undulate—to move in waves

unearth—to dig up

unequivocal—clear

unfaltering—unhesitating

unfathomable—not understandable

ungainly—awkward

unguent—an ointment

unimpeachable—undoubtable; above reproach

unique—unlike any other

unkempt—untidy

unmitigated—unrelieved

unprecedented—never having occurred before

unremitting—not letting up

unruly—unmanageable

unseemly—not proper

untenable—unable to be held

unwitting—unconscious; unaware

unwonted—rare

upbraid—to rebuke

urbane—polished and refined

usurp—to take by force

usury—lending money at outrageously high interest rates

utilitarian—useful

utopian—idealistic; perfect

uxorious—overly fond of one's wife

V

vacillate—to move one way and then the other; to waver

vacuous—empty; stupid

vagary—a peculiarity

vainglorious—vain and boastful

valiant—brave

validate—to confirm legally

vanguard—the group in front

vapid—dull

variegated—having a variety of colors in splotches; diverse

vaunt—a boast

veer—to change direction

vegetate—to have a dull, inactive existence

vehement—having great force or passion

venal—bribable

vendetta—a feud

vendor—a seller

vengeance—punishment; revenge

vencer—a thin covering of fine wood over cheaper wood; a thin and superficial display of a noble quality

venerable—old and honorable

venerate—to respect deeply

venial—forgivable

vent—to allow (steam or feelings) to escape

veracious—truthful

verbatim—word-for-word

verbiage—wordiness

verbose—wordy

verdant—green

verily—truly

verisimilar—appearing to be true

verity—truth

vernacular—the common speech of an area or its people

versatile—changeable; adaptable

vertigo—dizziness

vestige—a trace

viable—able or likely to live

viand—something to eat

vicarious—substitute; done or experienced by one person through another

vicissitudes—changes

victuals—food

vie—to compete

vigilant—watchful

vilify—to slander

vindicate—to free of blame

vindictive—seeking revenge

virile—manly; masculine

virtuoso—a skilled performer

virulent—deadly

visage—one's face

viscid—sticky; viscous

viscous—sticky; viscid

visionary—like a vision; unrealistic

vitiate—to spoil or debase

vitriolic—bitter

vituperation—harsh language

vivacious—lively

vivid—lively; intense

vociferous—loud

volatile—turning to vapor quickly; changeable

volition—employing one's will

voluble—talkative

voluptuous—sensual; inclined toward luxury

voracious—greedy

votary—one who has taken a vow; a follower or supporter of a cause

vouchsafe—to grant

vulnerable—in a position to be attacked or injured

W

waggish—playful

waive—to give up (a right, etc.)

wan—pale

wane—to decrease

wanton—morally loose; unwarranted

warranty—a guarantee

wary—cautious

wastrel—one who wastes (money)

weal—welfare

wheedle—to coax

whet—to sharpen

whimsical—fanciful

whit—(the) least bit

wily—sly

windfall—a surprising bit of good luck

winnow—to pick out the good elements or parts of something

winsome—charming

witless—foolish

witticism—a clever remark

wizened—withered; dried up

wont—accustomed

wraith—a ghost

wreak—to allow to be expressed; to inflict

wrest—to take away by force

wry—twisted; stubborn

Y

yeoman—a man who has a small
  amount of land

Z

zany—clownish; crazy

zealot—one who is extremely
  devoted to his cause

zenith—the highest point

zephyr—a breeze

zest—spirited enjoyment

FIFTY VOCABULARY PRACTICE TESTS OF ONE THOUSAND WORDS WHOSE MEANINGS YOU SHOULD KNOW

The 1000 words (in capital letters) in the following Practice Tests have been carefully selected. You should know the meanings of these words since many of them appear frequently in passages such as those you will encounter in the Critical Reading test.

Vocabulary Test 1

1. OBNOXIOUS
   (A) dreamy
   (B) visible
   (C) angry
   (D) daring
   (E) objectionable

2. VERBATIM
   (A) word for word
   (B) at will
   (C) without fail
   (D) in secret
   (E) in summary

3. ENTICE
   (A) inform
   (B) observe
   (C) permit
   (D) attract
   (E) disobey

4. ACCLAIM
   (A) discharge
   (B) excel
   (C) applaud
   (D) divide
   (E) speed

5. TURBULENCE
   (A) treachery
   (B) commotion
   (C) fear
   (D) triumph
   (E) overflow

6. DEFER
   (A) discourage
   (B) postpone
   (C) empty
   (D) minimize
   (E) estimate

7. ADAGE
   (A) proverb
   (B) supplement
   (C) tool
   (D) youth
   (E) hardness

8. ENSUE
   (A) compel
   (B) remain
   (C) absorb
   (D) plead
   (E) follow

9. ZENITH
   (A) lowest point
   (B) compass
   (C) summit
   (D) middle
   (E) wind direction

10. HYPOTHETICAL
    (A) magical
    (B) visual
    (C) two-faced
    (D) theoretical
    (E) excitable

11. SUPERFICIAL
    (A) shallow
    (B) unusually fine
    (C) proud
    (D) aged
    (E) spiritual

12. DISPARAGE
    (A) separate
    (B) compare
    (C) refuse
    (D) belittle
    (E) imitate

13. PROTAGONIST
    (A) prophet
    (B) explorer
    (C) talented child
    (D) convert
    (E) leading character

14. LUDICROUS
    (A) profitable
    (B) excessive
    (C) disordered
    (D) ridiculous
    (E) undesirable

15. INTREPID
    (A) moist
    (B) tolerant
    (C) fearless
    (D) rude
    (E) gay

16. FILCH
    (A) hide
    (B) swindle
    (C) drop
    (D) steal
    (E) covet

17. URBANE
    (A) well-dressed
    (B) polished
    (C) rural
    (D) friendly
    (E) prominent

18. DECANT
    (A) bisect
    (B) speak wildly
    (C) bequeath
    (D) pour off
    (E) abuse verbally

19. ANTITHESIS
    (A) contrast
    (B) conclusion
    (C) resemblance
    (D) examination
    (E) dislike

20. HERETICAL
    (A) heathenish
    (B) impractical
    (C) quaint
    (D) rash
    (E) unorthodox

Vocabulary Test 2

1. IMPROMPTU
   (A) offhand
   (B) laughable
   (C) fascinating
   (D) rehearsed
   (E) deceptive

2. CHIVALROUS
   (A) crude
   (B) military
   (C) handsome
   (D) foreign
   (E) courteous

3. HAVOC
   (A) festival
   (B) disease
   (C) ruin
   (D) sea battle
   (E) satchel

4. REJUVENATE
   (A) reply
   (B) renew
   (C) age
   (D) judge
   (E) reconsider

5. STILTED
   (A) stiffly formal
   (B) talking much
   (C) secretive
   (D) fashionable
   (E) senseless

6. SOLILOQUY
   (A) figure of speech
   (B) historical incident
   (C) monologue
   (D) isolated position
   (E) contradiction

7. AFFABLE
   (A) monotonous
   (B) affected
   (C) wealthy
   (D) sociable
   (E) selfish

8. NEBULOUS
   (A) subdued
   (B) eternal
   (C) dewy
   (D) cloudy
   (E) careless

9. STEREOTYPED
   (A) lacking originality
   (B) illuminating
   (C) pictorial
   (D) free from disease
   (E) sparkling

10. STUPEFY
    (A) lie
    (B) talk nonsense
    (C) bend
    (D) make dull
    (E) overeat

11. SAGE
    (A) wise man
    (B) tropical tree
    (C) tale
    (D) era
    (E) fool

12. ADMONISH
    (A) polish
    (B) escape
    (C) worship
    (D) distribute
    (E) caution

13. BESET
    (A) plead
    (B) perplex
    (C) pertain to
    (D) deny
    (E) caution

14. FIGMENT
    (A) ornamental openwork
    (B) perfume
    (C) undeveloped
    (D) statuette
    (E) invention

15. GLIB
    (A) dull
    (B) thin
    (C) weak
    (D) fluent
    (E) sharp

16. COALESCE
    (A) associate
    (B) combine
    (C) contact
    (D) conspire
    (E) cover

17. QUACK
    (A) clown
    (B) philanthropist
    (C) jester
    (D) dressmaker
    (E) charlatan

18. GAUCHE
    (A) clumsy
    (B) stupid
    (C) feeble-minded
    (D) impudent
    (E) foreign

19. REDUNDANT
    (A) necessary
    (B) plentiful
    (C) sufficient
    (D) diminishing
    (E) superfluous

20. ATROPHY
    (A) lose leaves
    (B) soften
    (C) waste away
    (D) grow
    (E) spread

Vocabulary Test 3

1. COMPREHEND
   (A) agree
   (B) settle
   (C) decide
   (D) reprieve
   (E) understand

2. ARDENT
   (A) eager
   (B) silvery
   (C) difficult
   (D) youthful
   (E) argumentative

3. EPITAPH
   (A) witty saying
   (B) satirical poem
   (C) concluding speech
   (D) seat beside a wall
   (E) inscription on a tomb

4. BEFIT
   (A) assist
   (B) suit
   (C) slander
   (D) stretch
   (E) effect

5. HABITAT
   (A) routine
   (B) carriage
   (C) long-term resident
   (D) dwelling place
   (E) article of clothing

6. REVERBERATE
   (A) uncover
   (B) blame
   (C) resound
   (D) regain
   (E) restore to life

7. PRECEDENCE
   (A) procession
   (B) impulsiveness
   (C) formality
   (D) priority
   (E) hesitation

8. SUFFICE
   (A) endure
   (B) annex
   (C) be foolish
   (D) be adequate
   (E) eat up

9. PERTINENT
   (A) convincing
   (B) applicable
   (C) habitual
   (D) foolproof
   (E) careful

10. TEMPESTUOUS
    (A) violent
    (B) short-lived
    (C) hard-hearted
    (D) heated
    (E) outrageous

11. VEHEMENT
    (A) thorough
    (B) unexpected
    (C) forceful
    (D) smooth-running
    (E) airy

12. REMUNERATION
    (A) understanding
    (B) finality
    (C) indebtedness
    (D) protest
    (E) compensation

13. FRIVOLITY
    (A) lightness
    (B) irritability
    (C) falseness
    (D) ornamentation
    (E) impurity

14. AURA
    (A) bitterness
    (B) delight
    (C) part of the ear
    (D) prophet
    (E) distinctive atmosphere

15. PERSONABLE
    (A) self-centered
    (B) attractive
    (C) insulting
    (D) intimate
    (E) sensitive

16. RESILIENCE
    (A) submission
    (B) elasticity
    (C) vigor
    (D) determination
    (E) recovery

17. ANALOGY
    (A) similarity
    (B) transposition
    (C) variety
    (D) distinction
    (E) appropriateness

18. FACETIOUS
    (A) obscene
    (B) shrewd
    (C) impolite
    (D) complimentary
    (E) witty

19. DIATRIBE
    (A) debate
    (B) monologue
    (C) oration
    (D) tirade
    (E) conversation

20. MALEDICTION
    (A) curse
    (B) mispronunciation
    (C) grammatical error
    (D) tactless remark
    (E) epitaph

Vocabulary Test 4

1. INTRIGUE
   - (A) request
   - (B) plot
   - (C) veto
   - (D) poison
   - (E) trespass

2. EXPLICIT
   - (A) violent
   - (B) incomplete
   - (C) forgotten
   - (D) lengthy
   - (E) definite

3. CEDE
   - (A) force
   - (B) stop
   - (C) yield
   - (D) keep
   - (E) warn

4. STEALTHY
   - (A) disobedient
   - (B) slender
   - (C) discontented
   - (D) sly
   - (E) vulgar

5. DAUNTLESS
   - (A) lazy
   - (B) poor
   - (C) bold
   - (D) modest
   - (E) uncivilized

6. DEBONAIR
   - (A) gay
   - (B) corrupt
   - (C) fragile
   - (D) extravagant
   - (E) healthful

7. JARGON
   - (A) unintelligible speech
   - (B) kind of gait
   - (C) word game
   - (D) exaggeration
   - (E) misinformation

8. PONDEROUS
   - (A) conceited
   - (B) shameful
   - (C) fearful
   - (D) heavy
   - (E) abundant

9. AMNESTY
   - (A) loss of memory
   - (B) ill will
   - (C) general pardon
   - (D) indistinctness
   - (E) improvement

10. DELETE
    - (A) injure
    - (B) delay
    - (C) please
    - (D) erase
    - (E) reveal

11. PILFER
   - (A) drain
   - (B) pray
   - (C) steal
   - (D) laugh
   - (E) toy with

12. CHAGRIN
   - (A) delight
   - (B) deceit
   - (C) wit
   - (D) caution
   - (E) vexation

13. DEFAMATION
   - (A) slander
   - (B) debt
   - (C) infection
   - (D) embezzlement
   - (E) deterioration

14. SUNDRY
   - (A) quiet
   - (B) various
   - (C) luxurious
   - (D) cheerless
   - (E) brittle

15. PALATIAL
   - (A) tasty
   - (B) magnificent
   - (C) disordered
   - (D) extreme
   - (E) secure

16. AGGREGATE
   - (A) result
   - (B) difference
   - (C) quotient
   - (D) product
   - (E) sum

17. APLOMB
   - (A) caution
   - (B) timidity
   - (C) self-assurance
   - (D) shortsightedness
   - (E) self-restraint

18. THERAPEUTIC
   - (A) curative
   - (B) restful
   - (C) warm
   - (D) stimulating
   - (E) professional

19. TRANSMUTE
   - (A) remove
   - (B) change
   - (C) duplicate
   - (D) carry
   - (E) explain

20. ATTRITION
   - (A) annihilation
   - (B) encirclement
   - (C) counter attack
   - (D) appeasement
   - (E) wearing down

Vocabulary Test 5

1. FORTITUDE
   (A) wealth
   (B) courage
   (C) honesty
   (D) loudness
   (E) luck

2. ABOLITION
   (A) retirement
   (B) disgust
   (C) enslavement
   (D) unrestricted power
   (E) complete destruction

3. LABYRINTH
   (A) pool
   (B) maze
   (C) formula
   (D) monster
   (E) song

4. MAIM
   (A) heal
   (B) disable
   (C) outwit
   (D) murder
   (E) bury

5. CRESTFALLEN
   (A) haughty
   (B) dejected
   (C) fatigued
   (D) disfigured
   (E) impolite

6. CUISINE
   (A) headdress
   (B) game of chance
   (C) leisurely voyage
   (D) artistry
   (E) style of cooking

7. CENSURE
   (A) erase
   (B) build up
   (C) criticize adversely
   (D) charm
   (E) help

8. DEVIATE
   (A) destroy
   (B) lower in value
   (C) invent
   (D) stray
   (E) depress

9. SWARTHY
   (A) dark-complexioned
   (B) slender
   (C) grass-covered
   (D) springy
   (E) rotating

10. MERCENARY
    (A) poisonous
    (B) unworthy
    (C) serving only for pay
    (D) luring by false charms
    (E) showing pity

11. EXHILARATION
    (A) animation
    (B) withdrawal
    (C) payment
    (D) suffocation
    (E) despair

12. RASPING
    (A) irritating
    (B) scolding
    (C) fastening
    (D) sighing
    (E) plundering

13. PROPONENT
    (A) spendthrift
    (B) rival
    (C) distributor
    (D) advocate
    (E) neighbor

14. REDUNDANT
    (A) flooded
    (B) dreadful
    (C) aromatic
    (D) excessive
    (E) reclining

15. DESULTORY
    (A) humid
    (B) envious
    (C) living in seclusion
    (D) involving a choice
    (E) aimless

16. TRUNCATE
    (A) divide equally
    (B) end swiftly
    (C) cut off
    (D) act cruelly
    (E) cancel

17. OSCILLATE
    (A) confuse
    (B) kiss
    (C) turn
    (D) vibrate
    (E) whirl

18. INOCULATE
    (A) make harmless
    (B) infect
    (C) cure
    (D) overcome
    (E) darken

19. PERUSAL
    (A) approval
    (B) estimate
    (C) reading
    (D) translation
    (E) computation

20. QUERULOUS
    (A) peculiar
    (B) fretful
    (C) inquisitive
    (D) shivering
    (E) annoying

Vocabulary Test 6

1. ACUTE
   (A) keen
   (B) bitter
   (C) brisk
   (D) genuine
   (E) certain

2. CLIENTELE
   (A) legal body
   (B) customers
   (C) board of directors
   (D) servants
   (E) tenants

3. SUCCUMB
   (A) follow
   (B) help
   (C) respond
   (D) yield
   (E) overthrow

4. SLOTH
   (A) selfishness
   (B) hatred
   (C) laziness
   (D) misery
   (E) slipperiness

5. INFRINGE
   (A) enrage
   (B) expand
   (C) disappoint
   (D) weaken
   (E) trespass

6. UNCANNY
   (A) ill-humored
   (B) immature
   (C) weird
   (D) unrestrained
   (E) insincere

7. SUBMISSIVE
   (A) unintelligent
   (B) underhanded
   (C) destructive
   (D) enthusiastic
   (E) meek

8. PEER
   (A) ancestor
   (B) teacher
   (C) judge
   (D) equal
   (E) assistant

9. EULOGIZE
   (A) kill
   (B) apologize
   (C) glorify
   (D) soften
   (E) imitate

10. INNOVATION
    (A) change
    (B) prayer
    (C) hint
    (D) restraint
    (E) inquiry

11. BEGUILE
    (A) cheapen
    (B) underestimate
    (C) charm
    (D) sympathize
    (E) forgive

12. AVID
    (A) lighthearted
    (B) eager
    (C) cautious
    (D) insincere
    (E) fast-moving

13. OMNIVOROUS
    (A) devouring everything
    (B) many-sided
    (C) powerful
    (D) living on plants
    (E) all-knowing

14. APPEND
    (A) rely
    (B) recognize
    (C) arrest
    (D) divide
    (E) attach

15. STRATEGEM
    (A) sneak attack
    (B) military command
    (C) thin layer
    (D) deceptive device
    (E) narrow passage

16. AUTONOMY
    (A) tyranny
    (B) independence
    (C) plebiscite
    (D) minority
    (E) dictatorship

17. MACHINATIONS
    (A) inventions
    (B) ideas
    (C) mysteries
    (D) plots
    (E) alliances

18. SCHISM
    (A) government
    (B) religion
    (C) division
    (D) combination
    (E) coalition

19. PUSILLANIMOUS
    (A) cowardly
    (B) extraordinary
    (C) ailing
    (D) evil-intentioned
    (E) excitable

20. TERMINOLOGY
    (A) technicality
    (B) finality
    (C) formality
    (D) explanation
    (E) nomenclature

Vocabulary Test 7

1. COLLABORATE
   (A) condense
   (B) converge
   (C) arrange in order
   (D) provide proof
   (E) act jointly

2. FUTILITY
   (A) uselessness
   (B) timelessness
   (C) stinginess
   (D) happiness
   (E) indistinctness

3. INTACT
   (A) blunt
   (B) fashionable
   (C) hidden
   (D) uninjured
   (E) attentive

4. FERVOR
   (A) originality
   (B) justice
   (C) zeal
   (D) productivity
   (E) corruption

5. UNERRING
   (A) modest
   (B) illogical
   (C) ghostly
   (D) matchless
   (E) unfailing

6. REFUTE
   (A) polish
   (B) disprove
   (C) throw away
   (D) break up
   (E) shut out

7. CONSENSUS
   (A) steadfastness of purpose
   (B) general agreement
   (C) lack of harmony
   (D) informal vote
   (E) impressive amount

8. COMPLIANT
   (A) tangled
   (B) grumbling
   (C) self-satisfied
   (D) treacherous
   (E) submissive

9. ACCESS
   (A) agreement
   (B) rapidity
   (C) welcome
   (D) approach
   (E) surplus

10. PRUDENT
    (A) wise
    (B) overcritical
    (C) famous
    (D) dull
    (E) early

11. INCUR
    (A) take to heart
    (B) anticipate
    (C) bring down on oneself
    (D) impress by repetition
    (E) attack

12. CAUSTIC
    (A) solemn
    (B) puzzling
    (C) biting
    (D) influential
    (E) attentive

13. DILATE
    (A) retard
    (B) fade
    (C) wander
    (D) expand
    (E) startle

14. APATHY
    (A) fixed dislike
    (B) skill
    (C) sorrow
    (D) lack of feeling
    (E) discontent

15. ELICIT
    (A) draw forth
    (B) cross out
    (C) run away
    (D) lengthen
    (E) revise

16. STIPEND
    (A) increment
    (B) bonus
    (C) commission
    (D) gift
    (E) salary

17. LITIGATION
    (A) publication
    (B) argument
    (C) endeavor
    (D) lawsuit
    (E) ceremony

18. FIASCO
    (A) disappointment
    (B) turning point
    (C) loss
    (D) celebration
    (E) complete failure

19. VAGARY
    (A) caprice
    (B) confusion
    (C) extravagance
    (D) loss of memory
    (E) shiftlessness

20. GRAPHIC
    (A) serious
    (B) concise
    (C) short
    (D) detailed
    (E) newsworthy

Vocabulary Test 8

1. APPEASE
   (A) attack
   (B) soothe
   (C) pray for
   (D) estimate
   (E) confess

2. RUTHLESS
   (A) senseless
   (B) sinful
   (C) ruddy
   (D) pitiless
   (E) degrading

3. MUSTER
   (A) rebel
   (B) mask
   (C) gather
   (D) dampen
   (E) grumble

4. ABDUCT
   (A) embarrass
   (B) desert
   (C) omit
   (D) kidnap
   (E) resign

5. KNOLL
   (A) elf
   (B) mound
   (C) bell
   (D) development
   (E) technique

6. IRATE
   (A) evil
   (B) wandering
   (C) repetitious
   (D) colorful
   (E) angry

7. GRIMACE
   (A) peril
   (B) subtle suggestion
   (C) signal
   (D) wry face
   (E) impurity

8. ACME
   (A) layer
   (B) summit
   (C) edge
   (D) pit
   (E) interval

9. COVENANT
   (A) solemn agreement
   (B) formal invitation
   (C) religious ceremony
   (D) general pardon
   (E) hiding place

10. APPALL
    (A) honor
    (B) decorate
    (C) calm
    (D) bore
    (E) dismay

11. JUDICIOUS
    (A) wise
    (B) dignified
    (C) lighthearted
    (D) confused
    (E) respectful

12. UNSCATHED
    (A) unashamed
    (B) uninjured
    (C) unskilled
    (D) unsuccessful
    (E) unconscious

13. CHIDE
    (A) misbehave
    (B) cool
    (C) select
    (D) conceal
    (E) scold

14. CHARLATAN
    (A) scholar
    (B) acrobat
    (C) quack
    (D) faithful
    (E) fast talker

15. DISBURSE
    (A) remove forcibly
    (B) twist
    (C) amuse
    (D) vary slightly
    (E) pay out

16. CONNOTATION
    (A) implication
    (B) footnote
    (C) deviation
    (D) comment
    (E) definition

17. TORTUOUS
    (A) crooked
    (B) difficult
    (C) painful
    (D) impassable
    (E) slow

18. FULMINATING
    (A) throbbing
    (B) pointed
    (C) wavelike
    (D) thundering
    (E) bubbling

19. CIRCUMVENT
    (A) freshen
    (B) change
    (C) control
    (D) harass
    (E) avoid

20. CARTEL
    (A) syndicate
    (B) world government
    (C) industrial pool
    (D) skilled craft
    (E) instrument of credit

Vocabulary Test 9

1. PARAMOUNT
   (A) equal
   (B) supreme
   (C) well-known
   (D) difficult
   (E) ready

2. BROCHURE
   (A) heavy shoe
   (B) weapon
   (C) pamphlet
   (D) roaster
   (E) ornament

3. FIDELITY
   (A) happiness
   (B) bravery
   (C) prosperity
   (D) hardness
   (E) loyalty

4. DIFFUSE
   (A) explain
   (B) scatter
   (C) differ
   (D) congeal
   (E) dart

5. AGGRESSIVE
   (A) disgusting
   (B) impulsive
   (C) short-sighted
   (D) coarse-grained
   (E) self-assertive

6. AMASS
   (A) accumulate
   (B) encourage
   (C) comprehend
   (D) blend
   (E) astonish

7. DIABOLIC
   (A) puzzling
   (B) uneducated
   (C) ornamental
   (D) fiendish
   (E) spinning

8. FORBEARANCE
   (A) rejection
   (B) forgetfulness
   (C) sensitivity
   (D) patience
   (E) expectation

9. TAINT
   (A) snarl
   (B) infect
   (C) unite
   (D) annoy
   (E) list

10. DISGRUNTLED
    (A) untidy
    (B) rambling
    (C) disabled
    (D) cheating
    (E) displeased

11. ANTIPATHY
   (A) exact opposite
   (B) intense dislike
   (C) high praise
   (D) tolerance
   (E) preventive medicine

12. HOMOGENEOUS
   (A) numerous
   (B) healthful
   (C) similar
   (D) assorted
   (E) educational

13. ARCHIVES
   (A) public records
   (B) models
   (C) supporting columns
   (D) tombs
   (E) large ships

14. INFAMY
   (A) anger
   (B) truth
   (C) disgrace
   (D) weakness
   (E) excitement

15. IMPINGE
   (A) swear
   (B) involve
   (C) erase
   (D) encroach
   (E) beg

16. PROLIFIC
   (A) meager
   (B) obedient
   (C) fertile
   (D) hardy
   (E) scanty

17. ASSUAGE
   (A) create
   (B) ease
   (C) enlarge
   (D) prohibit
   (E) rub out

18. DECORUM
   (A) wit
   (B) charm
   (C) adornment
   (D) seemliness
   (E) charity

19. PHLEGMATIC
   (A) tolerant
   (B) careless
   (C) sensitive
   (D) indifferent
   (E) sick

20. INTREPID
   (A) quick-witted
   (B) brutal
   (C) fearless
   (D) torrid
   (E) hearty

Vocabulary Test 10

1. PLACID
   (A) apparent
   (B) peaceful
   (C) wicked
   (D) unusual
   (E) absent-minded

2. EVASIVE
   (A) emotional
   (B) effective
   (C) destructive
   (D) empty
   (E) shifty

3. CHAOS
   (A) complete disorder
   (B) deep gorge
   (C) challenge
   (D) sudden attack
   (E) rejoicing

4. DESPICABLE
   (A) insulting
   (B) ungrateful
   (C) contemptible
   (D) unbearable
   (E) jealous

5. DERIDE
   (A) question
   (B) ignore
   (C) mock
   (D) unseat
   (E) produce

6. ELUDE
   (A) gladden
   (B) fascinate
   (C) mention
   (D) escape
   (E) ignore

7. MUTABLE
   (A) colorless
   (B) harmful
   (C) uniform
   (D) changeable
   (E) invisible

8. INDICATIVE
   (A) suggestive
   (B) curious
   (C) active
   (D) angry
   (E) certain

9. LEVITY
   (A) cleanness
   (B) tastiness
   (C) deadliness
   (D) sluggishness
   (E) lightness

10. EXCRUCIATING
    (A) disciplinary
    (B) screaming
    (C) torturing
    (D) offensive
    (E) outpouring

11. DEPOSE
    (A) lay bare
    (B) deprive of office
    (C) empty
    (D) behead
    (E) blemish

12. OSTENTATIOUS
    (A) unruly
    (B) showy
    (C) varied
    (D) scandalous
    (E) probable

13. CONCLAVE
    (A) private meeting
    (B) covered passage
    (C) solemn vow
    (D) curved surface
    (E) ornamental vase

14. FRAY
    (A) combat
    (B) trickery
    (C) unreality
    (D) madness
    (E) freedom

15. OBSESS
    (A) fatten
    (B) beset
    (C) make dull
    (D) exaggerate
    (E) interfere

16. ACTUATE
    (A) frighten
    (B) direct
    (C) isolate
    (D) dismay
    (E) impel

17. MOUNTEBANK
    (A) trickster
    (B) courier
    (C) scholar
    (D) cashier
    (E) pawnbroker

18. LACONIC
    (A) terse
    (B) informal
    (C) convincing
    (D) interesting
    (E) tedious

19. BOORISH
    (A) sporting
    (B) tiresome
    (C) argumentative
    (D) monotonous
    (E) rude

20. ERUDITE
    (A) modest
    (B) egotistical
    (C) learned
    (D) needless
    (E) experienced

Vocabulary Test 11

1. CHAFE
   (A) pretend
   (B) joke
   (C) drink deeply
   (D) irritate
   (E) lose courage

2. MISCONSTRUE
   (A) hate
   (B) destroy
   (C) misbehave
   (D) misinterpret
   (E) misplace

3. PHILANTHROPIST
   (A) student of language
   (B) collector of stamps
   (C) lover of mankind
   (D) seeker of truth
   (E) enemy of culture

4. CASTE
   (A) feudal system
   (B) division of society
   (C) political theory
   (D) method of punishment
   (E) monetary system

5. CHASTEN
   (A) punish
   (B) engrave
   (C) attract
   (D) trick
   (E) laugh at

6. CONDUCIVE
   (A) pardonable
   (B) identical
   (C) incidental
   (D) helpful
   (E) exceptional

7. SUBORDINATE
   (A) hostile
   (B) inferior
   (C) separate
   (D) earlier
   (E) adaptable

8. SUPERFLUOUS
   (A) inexact
   (B) excessive
   (C) insincere
   (D) excellent
   (E) unreal

9. WIELD
   (A) protect
   (B) handle
   (C) postpone
   (D) resign
   (E) unite

10. GARISH
    (A) showy
    (B) talkative
    (C) sleepy
    (D) thin
    (E) vine-covered

11. EQUITABLE
    (A) charitable
    (B) even-tempered
    (C) two-faced
    (D) undecided
    (E) just

12. AFFRONT
    (A) quarrel
    (B) fright
    (C) denial
    (D) boast
    (E) insult

13. EPOCH
    (A) heroic deed
    (B) legend
    (C) witty saying
    (D) period of time
    (E) summary

14. RETRIBUTION
    (A) donation
    (B) jealousy
    (C) intense education
    (D) slow withdrawal
    (E) punishment

15. ABASE
    (A) forgive
    (B) degrade
    (C) attach
    (D) take leave
    (E) cut off

16. ACRIMONIOUS
    (A) repulsive
    (B) enchanting
    (C) stinging
    (D) snobbish
    (E) disgusting

17. EMBRYONIC
    (A) hereditary
    (B) arrested
    (C) developed
    (D) functioning
    (E) rudimentary

18. INEXORABLE
    (A) unfavorable
    (B) permanent
    (C) crude
    (D) relentless
    (E) incomplete

19. PROTRACTED
    (A) boring
    (B) condensed
    (C) prolonged
    (D) comprehensive
    (E) measured

20. OBSEQUIOUS
    (A) courteous
    (B) fawning
    (C) respectful
    (D) overbearing
    (E) inexperienced

Vocabulary Test 12

1. MEANDER
   (A) grumble
   (B) wander aimlessly
   (C) come between
   (D) weigh carefully
   (E) sing

2. DESTITUTION
   (A) trickery
   (B) fate
   (C) lack of practice
   (D) recovery
   (E) extreme poverty

3. MALIGN
   (A) slander
   (B) prophesy
   (C) entreat
   (D) approve
   (E) praise

4. IMPOTENT
   (A) unwise
   (B) lacking strength
   (C) free of sin
   (D) without shame
   (E) commanding

5. SNIVEL
   (A) crawl
   (B) cut short
   (C) whine
   (D) doze
   (E) giggle

6. SOJOURN
   (A) court order
   (B) nickname
   (C) temporary stay
   (D) slip of the tongue
   (E) makeshift

7. PLATITUDE
   (A) home remedy
   (B) trite remark
   (C) balance wheel
   (D) rare animal
   (E) protective film

8. CONCORD
   (A) brevity
   (B) blame
   (C) kindness
   (D) worry
   (E) agreement

9. ABOMINABLE
   (A) hateful
   (B) ridiculous
   (C) untamed
   (D) mysterious
   (E) boastful

10. QUALM
    (A) sudden misgiving
    (B) irritation
    (C) cooling drink
    (D) deceit
    (E) attention to detail

11. CAREEN
    (A) celebrate
    (B) mourn
    (C) ridicule
    (D) lurch
    (E) beckon

12. CONVIVIAL
    (A) formal
    (B) gay
    (C) rotating
    (D) well-informed
    (E) insulting

13. RAMPANT
    (A) playful
    (B) crumbling
    (C) roundabout
    (D) unchecked
    (E) defensive

14. DOCILE
    (A) delicate
    (B) positive
    (C) dreary
    (D) obedient
    (E) melodious

15. VESTIGE
    (A) bone
    (B) test
    (C) entrance
    (D) cloak
    (E) trace

16. LOQUACIOUS
    (A) queer
    (B) logical
    (C) gracious
    (D) rural
    (E) talkative

17. PUGNACIOUS
    (A) bold
    (B) combative
    (C) brawny
    (D) pug-nosed
    (E) valiant

18. ASTRINGENT
    (A) bossy
    (B) musty
    (C) flexible
    (D) corrosive
    (E) contracting

19. ESCARPMENT
    (A) threat
    (B) limbo
    (C) cliff
    (D) behemoth
    (E) blight

20. AMENITIES
    (A) prayers
    (B) ceremonies
    (C) pageantries
    (D) pleasantries
    (E) social functions

Vocabulary Test 13

1. IMPEDIMENT
   (A) foundation
   (B) conceit
   (C) hindrance
   (D) luggage
   (E) instrument

2. ADHERE
   (A) pursue
   (B) control
   (C) arrive
   (D) cling
   (E) attend

3. COMPOSURE
   (A) sensitiveness
   (B) weariness
   (C) stylishness
   (D) hopefulness
   (E) calmness

4. PROVOCATION
   (A) sacred vow
   (B) formal announcement
   (C) cause of irritation
   (D) careful management
   (E) expression of disgust

5. SAVORY
   (A) thrifty
   (B) wise
   (C) appetizing
   (D) warm
   (E) uncivilized

6. CANDID
   (A) hidden
   (B) shining
   (C) straightforward
   (D) critical
   (E) warmhearted

7. ECLIPSE
   (A) stretch
   (B) obscure
   (C) glow
   (D) overlook
   (E) insert

8. CORRELATE
   (A) punish
   (B) wrinkle
   (C) conspire openly
   (D) give additional proof
   (E) connect systematically

9. INFIRMITY
   (A) disgrace
   (B) unhappiness
   (C) rigidity
   (D) hesitation
   (E) weakness

10. PALPITATE
    (A) faint
    (B) harden
    (C) throb
    (D) soothe
    (E) taste

11. IMPRUDENT
    (A) reckless
    (B) unexcitable
    (C) poor
    (D) domineering
    (E) powerless

12. DISSENSION
    (A) friction
    (B) analysis
    (C) swelling
    (D) injury
    (E) slyness

13. DISCONCERT
    (A) separate
    (B) cripple
    (C) lessen
    (D) upset
    (E) dismiss

14. RUDIMENTARY
    (A) discourteous
    (B) brutal
    (C) displeasing
    (D) elementary
    (E) embarrassing

15. AUTONOMOUS
    (A) self-governing
    (B) self-important
    (C) self-educated
    (D) self-explanatory
    (E) self-conscious

16. DEPLORE
    (A) condone
    (B) forget
    (C) forgive
    (D) deny
    (E) regret

17. BANAL
    (A) commonplace
    (B) flippant
    (C) pathetic
    (D) new
    (E) unexpected

18. ABACUS
    (A) casserole
    (B) blackboard
    (C) slide rule
    (D) adding device
    (E) long spear

19. SEISMISM
    (A) inundation
    (B) tide
    (C) volcano
    (D) earthquake
    (E) tornado

20. AMELIORATE
    (A) favor
    (B) improve
    (C) interfere
    (D) learn
    (E) straddle

Vocabulary Test 14

1. DEBRIS
   (A) sadness
   (B) decay
   (C) ruins
   (D) landslide
   (E) hindrance

2. CONSOLIDATE
   (A) show pity
   (B) strengthen
   (C) restrain
   (D) infect
   (E) use up

3. STAMINA
   (A) flatness
   (B) clearness
   (C) hesitation
   (D) vigor
   (E) reliability

4. FACET
   (A) phase
   (B) humor
   (C) story
   (D) discharge
   (E) assistance

5. INANIMATE
   (A) emotional
   (B) thoughtless
   (C) lifeless
   (D) inexact
   (E) silly

6. CALLOUS
   (A) frantic
   (B) misinformed
   (C) youthful
   (D) impolite
   (E) unfeeling

7. ENHANCE
   (A) sympathize
   (B) act out
   (C) weaken
   (D) make greater
   (E) fascinate

8. DISREPUTABLE
   (A) impolite
   (B) bewildered
   (C) debatable
   (D) unavailable
   (E) shameful

9. SEDATE
   (A) sober
   (B) seated
   (C) buried
   (D) drugged
   (E) timid

10. LUCRATIVE
    (A) lazy
    (B) coarse
    (C) profitable
    (D) brilliant
    (E) amusing

11. ASCERTAIN
    (A) hold fast
    (B) long for
    (C) declare
    (D) find out
    (E) avoid

12. LITERAL
    (A) flowery
    (B) matter-of-fact
    (C) sidewise
    (D) well-educated
    (E) firsthand

13. OSCILLATE
    (A) please
    (B) swing
    (C) purify
    (D) saturate
    (E) harden

14. CONCISE
    (A) accurate
    (B) brief
    (C) sudden
    (D) similar
    (E) painful

15. CONSTERNATION
    (A) restraint
    (B) close attention
    (C) dismay
    (D) self-importance
    (E) acknowledgment

16. CHARY
    (A) burned
    (B) careful
    (C) comfortable
    (D) fascinating
    (E) gay

17. CORPULENT
    (A) dead
    (B) fat
    (C) full
    (D) organized
    (E) similar

18. ENIGMA
    (A) ambition
    (B) foreigner
    (C) instrument
    (D) officer
    (E) riddle

19. INEPT
    (A) awkward
    (B) intelligent
    (C) ticklish
    (D) tawdry
    (E) uninteresting

20. INVETERATE
    (A) evil
    (B) habitual
    (C) inconsiderate
    (D) reformed
    (E) unintentional

Vocabulary Test 15

1. COLOSSAL
   (A) ancient
   (B) influential
   (C) destructive
   (D) dramatic
   (E) huge

2. EVICT
   (A) summon
   (B) excite
   (C) force out
   (D) prove
   (E) draw off

3. MISCHANCE
   (A) omission
   (B) ill luck
   (C) feeling of doubt
   (D) unlawful act
   (E) distrust

4. FELON
   (A) criminal
   (B) fugitive
   (C) traitor
   (D) coward
   (E) loafer

5. DEPLORE
   (A) empty
   (B) regret deeply
   (C) spread out
   (D) take an oath
   (E) omit

6. IMPLICIT
   (A) unquestioning
   (B) rude
   (C) relentless
   (D) sinful
   (E) daring

7. SLOVENLY
   (A) sleepy
   (B) tricky
   (C) untidy
   (D) moody
   (E) cowardly

8. EXTRANEOUS
   (A) familiar
   (B) unprepared
   (C) foreign
   (D) proper
   (E) utmost

9. IMPASSE
   (A) command
   (B) stubbornness
   (C) crisis
   (D) deadlock
   (E) failure

10. ABSOLVE
    (A) forgive
    (B) reduce
    (C) mix
    (D) deprive
    (E) detect

11. PROLETARIAT
    (A) revolutionists
    (B) intellectuals
    (C) slaves
    (D) laboring classes
    (E) landowners

12. REQUISITE
    (A) desirable
    (B) ridiculous
    (C) liberal
    (D) necessary
    (E) majestic

13. TENACIOUS
    (A) violent
    (B) given to arguing
    (C) slender
    (D) holding fast
    (E) menacing

14. SCINTILLATE
    (A) whirl
    (B) wander
    (C) scorch
    (D) sharpen
    (E) sparkle

15. PROPRIETY
    (A) success
    (B) cleverness
    (C) nearness
    (D) security
    (E) suitability

16. OBEISANCE
    (A) salary
    (B) justification
    (C) conduct
    (D) deference
    (E) forethought

17. PEDANTIC
    (A) stilted
    (B) odd
    (C) footworn
    (D) selfish
    (E) sincere

18. PETULANT
    (A) lazy
    (B) loving
    (C) patient
    (D) peevish
    (E) wary

19. PROCLIVITY
    (A) backwardness
    (B) edict
    (C) rainfall
    (D) slope
    (E) tendency

20. TRENCHANT
    (A) keen
    (B) good
    (C) edible
    (D) light
    (E) subterranean

Vocabulary Test 16

1. CUMBERSOME
   (A) habitual
   (B) clumsy
   (C) hasty
   (D) blameworthy
   (E) uneducated

2. CAPTIVATE
   (A) charm
   (B) dictate terms
   (C) overturn
   (D) find fault
   (E) hesitate

3. ZEALOUS
   (A) serious
   (B) speedy
   (C) flawless
   (D) necessary
   (E) enthusiastic

4. AROMATIC
   (A) shining
   (B) precise
   (C) ancient
   (D) fragrant
   (E) dry

5. RETROSPECT
   (A) careful inspection
   (B) reversal of form
   (C) review of the past
   (D) respect for authority
   (E) special attention

6. WHET
   (A) bleach
   (B) exhaust
   (C) harden
   (D) stimulate
   (E) question

7. CONTUSION
   (A) puzzle
   (B) shrinkage
   (C) bruise
   (D) uncleanness
   (E) fraud

8. COMPATIBLE
   (A) eloquent
   (B) adequate
   (C) overfed
   (D) comfortable
   (E) harmonious

9. CALLOUS
   (A) secretive
   (B) unruly
   (C) gloomy
   (D) unfeeling
   (E) hotheaded

10. REPUDIATE
    (A) reject
    (B) revalue
    (C) repay
    (D) forget
    (E) forgive

11. UNWITTING
    (A) undignified
    (B) unintentional
    (C) slack
    (D) obstinate
    (E) unaccustomed

12. ATTRIBUTE
    (A) quality
    (B) tax
    (C) desire
    (D) law
    (E) final sum

13. SCRUPULOUS
    (A) scornful
    (B) clean
    (C) frightening
    (D) doubting
    (E) conscientious

14. USURP
    (A) lend money
    (B) replace
    (C) murder
    (D) surrender
    (E) seize by force

15. CESSATION
    (A) witnessing
    (B) stopping
    (C) strain
    (D) leave-taking
    (E) unwillingness

16. VAPID
    (A) carefree
    (B) crazy
    (C) insipid
    (D) spotty
    (E) speedy

17. PROGNOSTICATE
    (A) forecast
    (B) ravish
    (C) salute
    (D) scoff
    (E) succeed

18. PROPRIETY
    (A) advancement
    (B) atonement
    (C) fitness
    (D) sobriety
    (E) use

19. PULCHRITUDE
    (A) beauty
    (B) character
    (C) generosity
    (D) intelligence
    (E) wickedness

20. SCRUPULOUS
    (A) drunken
    (B) ill
    (C) masterful
    (D) exact
    (E) stony

Vocabulary Test 17

1. RESOLUTE
   (A) determined
   (B) vibrating
   (C) irresistible
   (D) elastic
   (E) demanding

2. CRYSTALLIZE
   (A) glitter
   (B) give definite form to
   (C) chill
   (D) sweeten
   (E) polish vigorously

3. REGIME
   (A) ruler
   (B) military unit
   (C) form of government
   (D) contagion
   (E) guardian

4. LACERATED
   (A) unconscious
   (B) stitched
   (C) slender
   (D) raveled
   (E) mangled

5. AMISS
   (A) friendly
   (B) faulty
   (C) tardy
   (D) central
   (E) purposeless

6. INDOLENCE
   (A) poverty
   (B) laziness
   (C) danger
   (D) truth
   (E) attention

7. PRECARIOUS
   (A) trustful
   (B) early
   (C) previous
   (D) cautious
   (E) uncertain

8. CONNOISSEUR
   (A) investigator
   (B) government official
   (C) pretender
   (D) critical judge
   (E) portrait artist

9. HILARITY
   (A) wittiness
   (B) disobedience
   (C) mirth
   (D) heedlessness
   (E) contentment

10. EMIT
    (A) overlook
    (B) adorn
    (C) discharge
    (D) encourage
    (E) stress

11. AD INFINITUM
    (A) to a limit
    (B) from eternity
    (C) occasionally
    (D) endlessly
    (E) to the finish

12. EXTRICATE
    (A) disentangle
    (B) die out
    (C) praise
    (D) purify
    (E) argue with

13. SQUALID
    (A) dirty
    (B) unresponsive
    (C) wasteful
    (D) stormy
    (E) congested

14. COERCE
    (A) coincide
    (B) strengthen
    (C) accompany
    (D) compel
    (E) seek out

15. INTER
    (A) bury
    (B) stab
    (C) change
    (D) make peace
    (E) emphasize

16. INVARIABLE
    (A) diverse
    (B) eternal
    (C) fleeting
    (D) inescapable
    (E) uniform

17. VORACIOUS
    (A) excitable
    (B) honest
    (C) greedy
    (D) inclusive
    (E) circular

18. CONCENTRATE
    (A) agitate
    (B) protest
    (C) debate
    (D) harden
    (E) consolidate

19. PLAGIARIZE
    (A) annoy
    (B) borrow
    (C) steal ideas
    (D) imitate poorly
    (E) impede

20. CORTEGE
    (A) advisers
    (B) official papers
    (C) slaves
    (D) retinue
    (E) personal effects

Vocabulary Test 18

1. DYNAMIC
   (A) specialized
   (B) active
   (C) fragile
   (D) magical
   (E) comparative

2. ACHILLES' HEEL
   (A) source of strength
   (B) critical test
   (C) hereditary curse
   (D) vulnerable point
   (E) base conduct

3. AD LIB
   (A) cheerfully
   (B) freely
   (C) carefully
   (D) literally
   (E) wisely

4. DECRY
   (A) baffle
   (B) weep
   (C) trap
   (D) belittle
   (E) imagine

5. RAVAGE
   (A) ruin
   (B) tangle
   (C) delight
   (D) scold
   (E) crave

6. RENDEZVOUS
   (A) surrender
   (B) appointment
   (C) souvenir
   (D) hiding place
   (E) mutual exchange

7. SKULK
   (A) trail
   (B) shadow
   (C) ambush
   (D) lurk
   (E) race

8. COTERIE
   (A) formal farewell
   (B) trite remark
   (C) exclusive group
   (D) conclusive argument
   (E) good taste

9. NUPTIAL
   (A) moonlike
   (B) blunted
   (C) ritualistic
   (D) matrimonial
   (E) blessed

10. BALKED
    (A) swindled
    (B) thwarted
    (C) enlarged
    (D) waved
    (E) punished

11. CRESCENDO
    (A) increasing volume
    (B) decreasing tempo
    (C) abrupt ending
    (D) discordant note
    (E) musical composition

12. INDISCREET
    (A) unpopular
    (B) embarrassing
    (C) disloyal
    (D) unwise
    (E) greatly upset

13. UNWIELDY
    (A) stubborn
    (B) unhealthy
    (C) monotonous
    (D) shameful
    (E) clumsy

14. ENVISAGE
    (A) plot
    (B) conceal
    (C) wrinkle
    (D) contemplate
    (E) sneer

15. INTERIM
    (A) go-between
    (B) meantime
    (C) mixture
    (D) hereafter
    (E) period of rest

16. ANTIPATHY
    (A) sympathy
    (B) detachment
    (C) aversion
    (D) amazement
    (E) opposition

17. DEMUR
    (A) object
    (B) agree
    (C) murmur
    (D) discard
    (E) consider

18. PARAGON
    (A) dummy
    (B) lover
    (C) image
    (D) model
    (E) favorite

19. FINITE
    (A) impure
    (B) firm
    (C) minute
    (D) limited
    (E) unbounded

20. AUTARCHY
    (A) laissez-faire
    (B) motor-mindedness
    (C) pacifism
    (D) lawless confusion
    (E) self-government

Vocabulary Test 19

1. DISHEARTEN
   (A) shame
   (B) discourage
   (C) astound
   (D) disown
   (E) cripple

2. COMPONENT
   (A) memorial
   (B) pledge
   (C) convenience
   (D) ingredient
   (E) similarity

3. LURK
   (A) stagger
   (B) tempt
   (C) sneak
   (D) grin
   (E) rob

4. GRUDGING
   (A) impolite
   (B) dirty
   (C) hoarse
   (D) alarming
   (E) unwilling

5. SEMBLANCE
   (A) likeness
   (B) noise
   (C) foundation
   (D) glance
   (E) error

6. NETTLE
   (A) irritate
   (B) catch
   (C) accuse
   (D) make ill
   (E) fade away

7. TREMULOUS
   (A) slow
   (B) high-pitched
   (C) huge
   (D) shaking
   (E) spirited

8. TERSE
   (A) delicate
   (B) nervous
   (C) mild
   (D) numb
   (E) concise

9. AFFINITY
   (A) solemn declaration
   (B) indefinite amount
   (C) natural attraction
   (D) pain
   (E) wealth

10. VOLATILE
    (A) disobedient
    (B) changeable
    (C) forceful
    (D) willing
    (E) luxurious

11. CONJECTURE
    (A) work
    (B) joke
    (C) initiation
    (D) monument
    (E) guess

12. DAIS
    (A) platform
    (B) easy chair
    (C) waiting room
    (D) ornamental pin
    (E) figurehead

13.. IMPETUS
    (A) deadlock
    (B) collision
    (C) warning
    (D) wickedness
    (E) stimulus

14. INTROSPECTIVE
    (A) lacking strength
    (B) practicing self-examination
    (C) highly critical
    (D) intrusive
    (E) lacking confidence

15. DEIFY
    (A) describe
    (B) disobey
    (C) make presentable
    (D) worship as a god
    (E) challenge

16. DISCRIMINATION
    (A) acquittal
    (B) insight
    (C) caution
    (D) indiscretion
    (E) distortion

17. INVECTIVE
    (A) richness
    (B) goal
    (C) solemn oath
    (D) praise
    (E) verbal abuse

18. ADROIT
    (A) hostile
    (B) serene
    (C) pompous
    (D) skillful
    (E) allergic

19. LESION
    (A) injury
    (B) contortion
    (C) suffering
    (D) convulsion
    (E) aggravation

20. DILETTANTE
    (A) epicure
    (B) dabbler
    (C) procrastinator
    (D) literary genius
    (E) playboy

Vocabulary Test 20

1. HOMAGE
   (A) welcome
   (B) honor
   (C) coziness
   (D) criticism
   (E) regret

2. DISPERSE
   (A) restore
   (B) spread
   (C) grumble
   (D) soak
   (E) spend

3. RATIONAL
   (A) resentful
   (B) overjoyed
   (C) sensible
   (D) reckless
   (E) apologetic

4. RECLUSE
   (A) schemer
   (B) criminal
   (C) miser
   (D) adventurer
   (E) hermit

5. COMPLACENCY
   (A) tenderness
   (B) admiration
   (C) dependence
   (D) unity
   (E) self-satisfaction

6. MENACE
   (A) kill
   (B) threaten
   (C) waste
   (D) indicate
   (E) tease

7. DUPE
   (A) combine
   (B) reproduce
   (C) fool
   (D) grab
   (E) follow

8. ABATE
   (A) surprise
   (B) desert
   (C) decrease
   (D) humiliate
   (E) pay for

9. CONGENITAL
   (A) existing at birth
   (B) displaying weakness
   (C) related by marriage
   (D) overcrowded
   (E) unintelligent

10. INSURGENT
    (A) impractical
    (B) unbearable
    (C) overhanging
    (D) rebellious
    (E) patriotic

11. AGGREGATION
    (A) method
    (B) irritation
    (C) prize
    (D) collection
    (E) blessing

12. SUBLIME
    (A) exalted
    (B) underhanded
    (C) funny
    (D) conceited
    (E) secondary

13. POTENTATE
    (A) slave
    (B) soldier
    (C) adviser
    (D) informer
    (E) ruler

14. INTIMIDATE
    (A) frighten
    (B) suggest
    (C) dare
    (D) border upon
    (E) befriend

15. SARDONIC
    (A) decorative
    (B) polished
    (C) strange
    (D) fashionable
    (E) sarcastic

16. PROVISIONAL
    (A) military
    (B) tentative
    (C) absentee
    (D) democratic
    (E) appointed

17. CONDIMENT
    (A) ledger
    (B) ore
    (C) telegraph device
    (D) musical instrument
    (E) spice

18. RECALCITRANT
    (A) insincere
    (B) obstinate
    (C) crafty
    (D) conservative
    (E) reconcilable

19. BON MOT
    (A) witticism
    (B) pun
    (C) praise
    (D) last word
    (E) exact meaning

20. ACCOUTREMENTS
    (A) sealed orders
    (B) equipment
    (C) cartoons
    (D) correspondence
    (E) financial records

Vocabulary Test 21

1. ELECTRIFY
   (A) punish
   (B) improve
   (C) thrill
   (D) explain
   (E) investigate

2. DISCRETION
   (A) special privilege
   (B) individual judgment
   (C) unfair treatment
   (D) disagreement
   (E) embarrassment

3. GRAPPLE
   (A) dive
   (B) wrestle
   (C) handle
   (D) fit together
   (E) fondle

4. LAUDABLE
   (A) brave
   (B) comical
   (C) peaceful
   (D) praiseworthy
   (E) conspicuous

5. LONGEVITY
   (A) wisdom
   (B) length of life
   (C) society
   (D) system of measure
   (E) loudness

6. BLANCH
   (A) destroy
   (B) drink
   (C) whiten
   (D) feel
   (E) mend

7. SHREW
   (A) moneylender
   (B) fortune-teller
   (C) chronic invalid
   (D) unruly child
   (E) scolding woman

8. STALWART
   (A) diseased
   (B) feeble
   (C) needy
   (D) sturdy
   (E) truthful

9. APOGEE
   (A) rate of ascent
   (B) fortune-teller
   (C) measuring device
   (D) expression of regret
   (E) highest point

10. BANTER
    (A) tease playfully
    (B) strut boldly
    (C) ruin
    (D) bend slightly
    (E) relieve

11. GRANDIOSE
    (A) selfish
    (B) thankful
    (C) quarrelsome
    (D) elderly
    (E) impressive

12. INCONGRUOUS
    (A) indistinct
    (B) unsuitable
    (C) unimportant
    (D) illegal
    (E) inconvenient

13. PRONE
    (A) disposed
    (B) speechless
    (C) tardy
    (D) two-edged
    (E) quick

14. EMISSARY
    (A) rival
    (B) secret agent
    (C) master of ceremonies
    (D) refugee
    (E) clergyman

15. INVALIDATE
    (A) turn inward
    (B) deprive of force
    (C) mistrust
    (D) support with facts
    (E) neglect

16. HYPOTHESIS
    (A) assumption
    (B) proof
    (C) estimate
    (D) random guess
    (E) established truth

17. ALACRITY
    (A) slowness
    (B) indecision
    (C) caution
    (D) promptness
    (E) fearlessness

18. JETTISON
    (A) throw overboard
    (B) dismantle
    (C) scuttle
    (D) unload cargo
    (E) camouflage

19. VACILLATE
    (A) glitter
    (B) swerve
    (C) surrender
    (D) soften
    (E) waver

20. ASTUTE
    (A) shrewd
    (B) futile
    (C) potent
    (D) provocative
    (E) ruthless

Vocabulary Test 22

1. REPRESS
   (A) sharpen
   (B) restrain
   (C) repeat
   (D) disgust
   (E) grieve

2. BREACH
   (A) obstruction
   (B) violation
   (C) anticipation
   (D) accusation
   (E) decoration

3. DILIGENT
   (A) hesitant
   (B) prosperous
   (C) offensive
   (D) industrious
   (E) straightforward

4. CONCOCT
   (A) devise
   (B) link together
   (C) harmonize
   (D) meet privately
   (E) sweeten

5. FLAMBOYANT
   (A) scandalous
   (B) showy
   (C) nonsensical
   (D) manly
   (E) temporary

6. ECCENTRICITY
   (A) overabundance
   (B) self-consciousness
   (C) adaptability
   (D) publicity
   (E) oddity

7. VINDICTIVE
   (A) gloomy
   (B) cowardly
   (C) vengeful
   (D) cheerful
   (E) boastful

8. GRAPHIC
   (A) vivid
   (B) harsh-sounding
   (C) free from error
   (D) dignified
   (E) pliable

9. PLACARD
   (A) poster
   (B) souvenir
   (C) soothing medicine
   (D) exact reproduction
   (E) contemptuous remark

10. PUTREFY
    (A) scour
    (B) paralyze
    (C) rot
    (D) neglect
    (E) argue

11. CLEMENCY
    (A) purity
    (B) timidity
    (C) courage
    (D) simplicity
    (E) mildness

12. UNSCATHED
    (A) uninterested
    (B) unsettled
    (C) unspoken
    (D) unharmed
    (E) unknown

13. RELINQUISH
    (A) shrink from
    (B) take pity on
    (C) yield
    (D) lessen
    (E) recall

14. ALLAY
    (A) offend
    (B) suffer
    (C) resemble
    (D) assign
    (E) calm

15. ANIMOSITY
    (A) liveliness
    (B) worry
    (C) ill will
    (D) regret
    (E) sarcasm

16. PROVISO
    (A) final treaty
    (B) condition
    (C) demand
    (D) official document
    (E) proclamation

17. MACABRE
    (A) gruesome
    (B) meager
    (C) sordid
    (D) fantastic
    (E) cringing

18. AUGMENT
    (A) curtail
    (B) change
    (C) restore
    (D) conceal
    (E) increase

19. INTEGRAL
    (A) useful
    (B) powerful
    (C) essential
    (D) mathematical
    (E) indestructible

20. IMPUNITY
    (A) shamelessness
    (B) power of action
    (C) self-reliance
    (D) haughtiness
    (E) exemption from
        punishment

Vocabulary Test 23

1. SOLICIT
   (A) request
   (B) worry
   (C) command
   (D) deny
   (E) depend

2. PERTURB
   (A) pierce
   (B) filter
   (C) calculate
   (D) agitate
   (E) disregard

3. JAUNTY
   (A) bored
   (B) envious
   (C) quarrelsome
   (D) chatty
   (E) lively

4. DRIVEL
   (A) shrill laughter
   (B) foolish talk
   (C) untidy dress
   (D) waste matter
   (E) quaint humor

5. FRUGAL
   (A) sickly
   (B) saving
   (C) slow
   (D) chilled
   (E) frightened

6. IOTA
   (A) first step
   (B) sacred picture
   (C) ornamental scroll
   (D) crystalline substance
   (E) very small quantity

7. POACH
   (A) squander
   (B) trespass
   (C) outwit
   (D) bully
   (E) borrow

8. DEFECTION
   (A) delay
   (B) slander
   (C) respect
   (D) desertion
   (E) exemption

9. MASTICATE
   (A) chew
   (B) slaughter
   (C) ripen
   (D) enroll
   (E) tangle

10. ANALOGY
   (A) imitation
   (B) research
   (C) calendar
   (D) similarity
   (E) disagreement

11. GIRD
    (A) stare
    (B) thresh
    (C) encircle
    (D) complain
    (E) perforate

12. BIZARRE
    (A) charitable
    (B) joyous
    (C) flattering
    (D) insane
    (E) fantastic

13. PERENNIAL
    (A) superior
    (B) unceasing
    (C) notable
    (D) short-lived
    (E) authoritative

14. PROGENITOR
    (A) genius
    (B) wastrel
    (C) forefather
    (D) magician
    (E) publisher

15. EMBELLISH
    (A) organize
    (B) involve
    (C) rob
    (D) beautify
    (E) correct

16. LATENT
    (A) inherent
    (B) lazy
    (C) dormant
    (D) crushed
    (E) anticipated

17. OBDURATE
    (A) patient
    (B) stupid
    (C) rude
    (D) stubborn
    (E) tolerant

18. BIZARRE
    (A) boastful
    (B) warlike
    (C) sluggish
    (D) fantastic
    (E) oriental

19. ARROYO
    (A) cliff
    (B) plain
    (C) ranch
    (D) gully
    (E) cactus

20. AUGUR
    (A) enlarge
    (B) foretell
    (C) suggest
    (D) evaluate
    (E) minimize

Vocabulary Test 24

1. DILEMMA
   (A) punishment
   (B) division in ranks
   (C) ability to detect
   (D) perplexing choice
   (E) word with two meanings

2. CELESTIAL
   (A) musical
   (B) heavenly
   (C) stately
   (D) unmarried
   (E) aged

3. MILITANT
   (A) political
   (B) mighty
   (C) aggressive
   (D) peaceable
   (E) illegal

4. EMINENT
   (A) noted
   (B) moral
   (C) future
   (D) low
   (E) unwise

5. PERCEIVE
   (A) resolve
   (B) observe
   (C) organize
   (D) stick in
   (E) copy down

6. IDIOSYNCRASY
   (A) stupidity
   (B) virtue
   (C) personal peculiarity
   (D) foreign dialect
   (E) similarity

7. EDIFICE
   (A) tool
   (B) large building
   (C) garden
   (D) mushroom
   (E) set of books

8. SEEDY
   (A) dishonest
   (B) helpless
   (C) vague
   (D) nervous
   (E) shabby

9. SUPPLANT
   (A) spend
   (B) unite
   (C) recall
   (D) replace
   (E) purpose

10. DESIST
    (A) loiter
    (B) stand
    (C) hurry
    (D) stumble
    (E) stop

11. IMPLEMENT
   (A) carry out
   (B) fall apart
   (C) give freely
   (D) object strongly
   (E) praise highly

12. INSUBORDINATE
   (A) unreal
   (B) disobedient
   (C) inferior
   (D) unfaithful
   (E) unnecessary

13. ITINERANT
   (A) small
   (B) intensive
   (C) repetitive
   (D) wandering
   (E) begging

14. ADVERSITY
   (A) misfortune
   (B) surprise
   (C) economy
   (D) publicity
   (E) warning

15. DISSIPATE
   (A) explain
   (B) puzzle
   (C) rearrange
   (D) envy
   (E) waste

16. CONTRITE
   (A) infectious
   (B) worried
   (C) penitent
   (D) sympathetic
   (E) tolerant

17. OFFICIOUS
   (A) silly
   (B) gay
   (C) sarcastic
   (D) meddlesome
   (E) quarrelsome

18. PAEAN
   (A) prize
   (B) song of praise
   (C) decoration
   (D) certificate
   (E) story of heroism

19. EXOTIC
   (A) romantic
   (B) exciting
   (C) wealthy
   (D) strange
   (E) tropical

20. ARCHIPELAGO
   (A) slender isthmus
   (B) long, narrow land mass
   (C) string of lakes
   (D) high, flat plain
   (E) group of small islands

Vocabulary Test 25

1. CURRENTLY
   (A) at the present time
   (B) swiftly
   (C) commendably
   (D) smoothly
   (E) electrically

2. PARTICIPANT
   (A) a form of the verb
   (B) haste
   (C) sharer
   (D) weak player
   (E) very steep hill

3. INEVITABLE
   (A) not subject to evil
   (B) obscure
   (C) probable
   (D) unavoidable
   (E) harmful

4. INVINCIBLE
   (A) unable to be defended
   (B) undeniable
   (C) past help
   (D) unable to be conquered
   (E) very sharp

5. TENACITY
   (A) laziness
   (B) misfortune
   (C) persistency
   (D) poise
   (E) stability

6. FANATICISM
   (A) perplexity
   (B) endurance
   (C) remarkable power
   (D) idleness
   (E) excessive enthusiasm

7. CREVICE
   (A) scouting party
   (B) difficult travel
   (C) a tight squeeze
   (D) fissure
   (E) implement for digging

8. SAGELY
   (A) carelessly
   (B) mildly
   (C) tastefully
   (D) bitterly
   (E) wisely

9. CONCERTED
   (A) accompanied by music
   (B) disturbed
   (C) arranged by mutual consent
   (D) handled with care
   (E) cut short

10. OSTENSIBLY
    (A) apparently
    (B) meekly
    (C) cruelly
    (D) bravely
    (E) with hostility

11. UNCOMPROMISING
   (A) capable
   (B) unsuccessful
   (C) unwilling to make
      concessions
   (D) arranged in a conference
   (E) lacking in courage

12. COLLATERAL
   (A) something given as security
   (B) profitable enterprise
   (C) unnecessary help
   (D) steep slope
   (E) very wide board

13. CONSERVATIVE
   (A) exact
   (B) moderate
   (C) natural
   (D) unusual
   (E) deceptive

14. RETROSPECT
   (A) special kind of telescope
   (B) microscope
   (C) prism
   (D) review of the past
   (E) forecast of future events

15. DEVIATE
   (A) speak ill of
   (B) sap the life out of
   (C) turn from a course
   (D) turn upside down
   (E) injure

16. DESPICABLE
   (A) contemptible
   (B) poverty-stricken
   (C) destructible
   (D) peace-loving
   (E) without intelligence

17. INCITEMENT
   (A) commotion
   (B) exception
   (C) stimulation
   (D) duration
   (E) emotion

18. INCONTROVERTIBLE
   (A) not advisable
   (B) not accepted
   (C) steadfast
   (D) difficult to understand
   (E) not to be disputed

19. PROLETARIAN
   (A) politician
   (B) laborer
   (C) cruel tyrant
   (D) soldier
   (E) stupid fellow

20. COMPLEMENT
   (A) flattery
   (B) contempt
   (C) remuneration
   (D) tool
   (E) completing part

Vocabulary Test 26

1. INCESSANTLY
   (A) uncertainly
   (B) continuously
   (C) incidentally
   (D) universally
   (E) quickly

2. INTRICATE
   (A) involved
   (B) erect
   (C) remote
   (D) unjust
   (E) ignorant

3. DISSENTING
   (A) agreeing
   (B) fooling
   (C) withholding approval
   (D) annoying
   (E) removing odor

4. REFUTE
   (A) disobey
   (B) remove to a far point
   (C) offend
   (D) disprove
   (E) strike

5. POTENT
   (A) lacking strength
   (B) making a request
   (C) having power
   (D) soothing
   (E) perfumed

6. COMPLACENT
   (A) businesslike
   (B) obedient
   (C) self-satisfied
   (D) dishonest
   (E) careless

7. CYNICAL
   (A) poisonous
   (B) sneering
   (C) pleasure-loving
   (D) sinful
   (E) careless

8. DISPARAGE
   (A) belittle
   (B) declare unequal
   (C) separate
   (D) divide
   (E) dismiss

9. ANARCHY
   (A) government by one man
   (B) government by the rich
   (C) government by the poor
   (D) absence of government
   (E) hostility

10. PAYEE
    (A) one who becomes wealthy
    (B) debtor
    (C) banker
    (D) savage rodent
    (E) one to whom money is paid

11. TRADITIONAL
   (A) fundamental
   (B) customary
   (C) lasting
   (D) conclusive
   (E) old-fashioned

12. COMPULSION
   (A) force
   (B) tact
   (C) persuasion
   (D) bribery
   (E) sophistry

13. SINISTER
   (A) unmarried
   (B) black
   (C) evil
   (D) peculiar
   (E) discontented

14. NULLIFY
   (A) execute
   (B) destroy
   (C) establish
   (D) confirm
   (E) sustain

15. LONGEVITY
   (A) accomplishment
   (B) fame
   (C) good deed
   (D) sense of humor
   (E) long life

16. SURVEILLANCE
   (A) close watch
   (B) hiding
   (C) smoke screen
   (D) exact measuring
   (E) subordination

17. RENDITION
   (A) completion
   (B) mutilation
   (C) interpretation
   (D) hearing
   (E) overturning

18. PERMEATE
   (A) impress
   (B) permit
   (C) penetrate
   (D) imperil
   (E) conquer

19. INNOCUOUS
   (A) intact
   (B) harmless
   (C) spotless
   (D) trusting
   (E) childish

20. INCARCERATE
   (A) imperil
   (B) fine
   (C) torture
   (D) imprison
   (E) behead

Vocabulary Test 27

1. VAGUE
   (A) obscure
   (B) valuable
   (C) vivid
   (D) gray
   (E) real

2. SENTIMENTAL
   (A) criminal
   (B) romantic
   (C) consistent
   (D) morbid
   (E) fruitful

3. REGIME
   (A) summary
   (B) manner of rule
   (C) company of soldiers
   (D) opinion
   (E) stern commander

4. FEAT
   (A) duty
   (B) unusual injury
   (C) act
   (D) struggle
   (E) victory

5. JEOPARDIZE
   (A) offend
   (B) disgust
   (C) discourage
   (D) endanger
   (E) prolong

6. CONTROVERSY
   (A) long report
   (B) agreement
   (C) alternative
   (D) disputation
   (E) doubt

7. UNKEMPT
   (A) uncontrolled
   (B) inharmonious
   (C) unpretentious
   (D) crude
   (E) untidy

8. PANDEMONIUM
   (A) cure-all
   (B) collection
   (C) hatred
   (D) tumult
   (E) reptile

9. INTROSPECTION
   (A) self-examination
   (B) research
   (C) questionnaire
   (D) intrusion
   (E) self-assertion

10. STOLID
    (A) red
    (B) sunburned
    (C) sullen
    (D) pallid
    (E) dull

11. INFLEXIBLE
    (A) weak
    (B) righteous
    (C) harmless
    (D) unyielding
    (E) uneasy

12. SALVAGE
    (A) save
    (B) cut the edge of material
    (C) apply ointment
    (D) destroy
    (E) treat brutally

13. SUCCUMB
    (A) compromise
    (B) die
    (C) compete
    (D) besiege
    (E) conquer

14. PRECISION
    (A) fussiness
    (B) determination
    (C) accuracy
    (D) cutting
    (E) progress

15. CULT
    (A) mob
    (B) party
    (C) club
    (D) nation
    (E) sect

16. INTEGRITY
    (A) honesty
    (B) humor
    (C) knowledge
    (D) kindliness
    (E) courage

17. DOCILE
    (A) grateful
    (B) childish
    (C) sweet
    (D) obedient
    (E) adoring

18. RELENTLESS
    (A) stern
    (B) remorseful
    (C) exhausted
    (D) not difficult
    (E) insipid

19. CONSTERNATION
    (A) discontent
    (B) disappointment
    (C) disapproval
    (D) dismay
    (E) distrust

20. CAPITULATE
    (A) classify
    (B) reach up
    (C) cover
    (D) count
    (E) surrender

Vocabulary Test 28

1. ETHICS
   (A) religion
   (B) conduct
   (C) character
   (D) mathematics
   (E) moral principles

2. ZEALOUSNESS
   (A) earliness
   (B) firmness
   (C) earnestness
   (D) unwillingness
   (E) indifference

3. CLIENTELE
   (A) artists
   (B) classmates
   (C) friends
   (D) customers
   (E) scientists

4. CHRONOLOGY
   (A) perpetual calendar
   (B) conformed habit
   (C) time sequence
   (D) table of contents
   (E) prolonged suffering

5. ARTICULATION
   (A) accent
   (B) dialect
   (C) enunciation
   (D) pitch
   (E) impediment

6. AUTOCRATIC
   (A) democratic
   (B) yielding
   (C) resolute
   (D) dictatorial
   (E) motor-minded

7. OBSESSION
   (A) asset
   (B) fixed idea
   (C) main concern
   (D) idol
   (E) thought

8. VESTIGE
   (A) cause
   (B) garment
   (C) proof
   (D) symbol
   (E) trace

9. SUBVERSIVE
   (A) changeable
   (B) controversial
   (C) destructive
   (D) drowned
   (E) saucy

10. OBLOQUY
    (A) objection
    (B) result
    (C) wastefulness
    (D) greed
    (E) abuse

11. DETERIORATE
    (A) defend
    (B) delay
    (C) depreciate
    (D) originate
    (E) ornament

12. ADOLESCENT
    (A) carefree
    (B) worshipful
    (C) foolish
    (D) youthful
    (E) awkward

13. ANTAGONIST
    (A) opponent
    (B) killer
    (C) actor
    (D) trainer
    (E) underdog

14. DILUTE
    (A) chill
    (B) sweeten
    (C) sip
    (D) mix
    (E) weaken

15. PRETEXT
    (A) form
    (B) solution
    (C) excuse
    (D) course
    (E) result

16. CANDID
    (A) shifty
    (B) impudent
    (C) sweet
    (D) frank
    (E) bold

17. CONCUR
    (A) agree
    (B) beat
    (C) blame
    (D) happen
    (E) try

18. CAPITULATE
    (A) behead
    (B) creep
    (C) overturn
    (D) repeat
    (E) surrender

19. DOGMA
    (A) Bible study
    (B) personal opinion
    (C) free thought
    (D) statute
    (E) doctrine

20. ACUMEN
    (A) cupidity
    (B) honesty
    (C) hardness
    (D) craftiness
    (E) cleverness

Vocabulary Test 29

1. MELANCHOLY
   (A) awkward
   (B) disagreeable
   (C) gloomy
   (D) remote
   (E) haughty

2. VOGUE
   (A) elegance
   (B) fashion
   (C) attire
   (D) ambiguity
   (E) reputation

3. MASSIVE
   (A) autocratic
   (B) lavish
   (C) weighty
   (D) indispensable
   (E) destructive

4. ASPHYXIA
   (A) animation
   (B) prostration
   (C) despair
   (D) suffocation
   (E) loss of memory

5. USURP
   (A) imprison
   (B) insult
   (C) parade
   (D) seize
   (E) torture

6. COSMOS
   (A) breviary
   (B) comrade
   (C) forest
   (D) rogue
   (E) universe

7. EPIGRAM
   (A) obituary notice
   (B) balanced sentence
   (C) prophecy
   (D) pithy saying
   (E) exclamation

8. PROPHYLACTIC
   (A) causative
   (B) curative
   (C) toxic
   (D) preventive
   (E) sterile

9. GARRULOUS
   (A) queer
   (B) logical
   (C) gracious
   (D) rural
   (E) voluble

10. RESCIND
    (A) revoke
    (B) inflame
    (C) rescue
    (D) beg
    (E) request

11. FELONY
    (A) accusation
    (B) release
    (C) trial
    (D) companionship
    (E) crime

12. DECOY
    (A) amuse
    (B) exploit
    (C) forage
    (D) lure
    (E) brighten

13. DAZING
    (A) alarming
    (B) scolding
    (C) sleeping
    (D) whirling
    (E) stunning

14. ENTHUSIASTIC
    (A) ardent
    (B) appreciative
    (C) frank
    (D) fascinating
    (E) uneasy

15. GRAPPLE
    (A) grace
    (B) grind
    (C) grip
    (D) grovel
    (E) grumble

16. PROFOUND
    (A) faulty
    (B) deep
    (C) distinctive
    (D) authentic
    (E) unreasonable

17. EXODUS
    (A) request
    (B) departure
    (C) rebuke
    (D) journey
    (E) revelation

18. FATHOM
    (A) assay
    (B) budget
    (C) consider
    (D) understand
    (E) weight

19. LACONIC
    (A) concise
    (B) informal
    (C) convincing
    (D) interesting
    (E) tedious

20. INIQUITY
    (A) persecution
    (B) righteousness
    (C) wickedness
    (D) disparity
    (E) irregularity

Vocabulary Test 30

1. SKEPTICISM
   (A) awe
   (B) education
   (C) displeasure
   (D) opinion
   (E) doubt

2. DETOUR
   (A) swear
   (B) go around
   (C) wreck
   (D) let slip
   (E) turn back

3. CRUCIAL
   (A) painful
   (B) difficult
   (C) decisive
   (D) negligible
   (E) irritable

4. CALCULATE
   (A) compute
   (B) expect
   (C) investigate
   (D) multiply
   (E) specify

5. ESPIONAGE
   (A) perfidy
   (B) sabotage
   (C) spying
   (D) sedition
   (E) treachery

6. AMALGAMATE
   (A) confuse
   (B) disband
   (C) produce
   (D) unite
   (E) victimize

7. HYPOTHESIS
   (A) proof
   (B) assumption
   (C) estimate
   (D) random guess
   (E) established truth

8. INCALCULABLE
   (A) boundless
   (B) frugal
   (C) incompetent
   (D) nonessential
   (E) unreasonable

9. CAJOLE
   (A) banter
   (B) fondle
   (C) compliment
   (D) mislead
   (E) coax

10. PSALTERY
    (A) ledger
    (B) ore
    (C) telegraph device
    (D) spice
    (E) musical instrument

11. VERSATILE
    (A) all-round
    (B) awkward
    (C) poetic
    (D) unusual
    (E) wasteful

12. DORMANT
    (A) agile
    (B) inactive
    (C) docile
    (D) profound
    (E) unsocial

13. PROXY
    (A) agent
    (B) lawyer
    (C) promoter
    (D) referee
    (E) local magistrate

14. APTITUDE
    (A) height
    (B) donation
    (C) feeling
    (D) ability
    (E) knowledge

15. DELUGE
    (A) flood
    (B) loss
    (C) support
    (D) sympathy
    (E) trouble

16. FORTITUDE
    (A) completion
    (B) misfortune
    (C) pluck
    (D) success
    (E) truthfulness

17. SHEATH
    (A) belt
    (B) clothing
    (C) hook
    (D) linen
    (E) scabbard

18. ELECTORATE
    (A) nominee
    (B) office holder
    (C) group of voters
    (D) privileged class
    (E) defeated candidate

19. APPROXIMATION
    (A) amplitude
    (B) annuity
    (C) antecedent
    (D) approach
    (E) accumulation

20. ADROIT
    (A) allergic
    (B) hostile
    (C) pompous
    (D) serene
    (E) skillful

Vocabulary Test 31

1. AFFILIATE
   (A) associate
   (B) begin
   (C) communicate
   (D) compare
   (E) compete

2. DEFLATE
   (A) decorate
   (B) destroy
   (C) expand
   (D) peel
   (E) reduce

3. NONCHALANT
   (A) ignoble
   (B) inoffensive
   (C) mentally unsound
   (D) undecided
   (E) unruffled

4. RASH
   (A) merciless
   (B) quarrelsome
   (C) reckless
   (D) thunderstruck
   (E) vigorous

5. TYCOON
   (A) blusterer
   (B) bureaucrat
   (C) industrial magnate
   (D) statesman
   (E) strikebreaker

6. CAUSTIC
   (A) desultory
   (B) fallacious
   (C) reasonable
   (D) stinging
   (E) wearing

7. CACHE
   (A) box
   (B) cave
   (C) hiding place
   (D) restroom
   (E) wagon

8. AWRY
   (A) askew
   (B) deplorable
   (C) odd
   (D) simple
   (E) striking

9. CRUET
   (A) bottle
   (B) cake
   (C) napkin
   (D) plate
   (E) salad

10. RUTHLESS
    (A) widowed
    (B) masculine
    (C) bitter
    (D) cruel
    (E) toothless

11. ANTIDOTE
    (A) cure-all
    (B) diet
    (C) laxative
    (D) remedy
    (E) salve

12. AMICABLE
    (A) constant
    (B) friendly
    (C) pliable
    (D) tough
    (E) vigorous

13. DIVULGE
    (A) hide
    (B) muddle
    (C) reveal
    (D) suspect
    (E) understand

14. PASSIVE
    (A) helpful
    (B) impulsive
    (C) submissive
    (D) tired
    (E) treacherous

15. DETRIMENTAL
    (A) determined
    (B) forceful
    (C) injurious
    (D) potent
    (E) tactful

16. INCOHERENT
    (A) brief
    (B) disconnected
    (C) exaggerated
    (D) hasty
    (E) inadequate

17. MASTICATE
    (A) assimilate
    (B) chew
    (C) digest
    (D) liberate
    (E) slice

18. VERTICAL
    (A) curved
    (B) direct
    (C) flat
    (D) perpendicular
    (E) straight

19. CREDIBLE
    (A) believable
    (B) praiseworthy
    (C) readable
    (D) religious
    (E) understandable

20. VERACITY
    (A) truth
    (B) beauty
    (C) importance
    (D) luck
    (E) necessity

Vocabulary Test 32

1. DILEMMA
   (A) quarrel
   (B) denial
   (C) predicament
   (D) apparition
   (E) embarrassment

2. APPORTIONED
   (A) collected
   (B) saved
   (C) changed
   (D) distributed
   (E) accumulated

3. WRITHE
   (A) slip
   (B) sob
   (C) relax
   (D) resist
   (E) squirm

4. CALLOUS
   (A) flowerlike
   (B) harmful
   (C) pale
   (D) unfeeling
   (E) warm

5. MEDIOCRE
   (A) ordinary
   (B) confused
   (C) skillful
   (D) distraught
   (E) self-satisfied

6. FIDELITY
   (A) bank
   (B) loyalty
   (C) insurance
   (D) policy
   (E) valor

7. MOCK
   (A) injure
   (B) grieve
   (C) laugh
   (D) dull
   (E) taunt

8. MARTIAL
   (A) warlike
   (B) married
   (C) creative
   (D) unyielding
   (E) strict

9. TRANSCEND
   (A) translate
   (B) enjoy
   (C) strike out
   (D) surpass
   (E) climb

10. DISPUTATIOUS
    (A) odorous
    (B) argumentative
    (C) unclear
    (D) sour
    (E) overflowing

11. FICTITIOUS
    (A) difficult
    (B) imaginary
    (C) novel
    (D) ordinary
    (E) unknown

12. EPISODE
    (A) fable
    (B) incident
    (C) letter
    (D) postscript
    (E) reverie

13. SUFFICIENT
    (A) actual
    (B) adequate
    (C) real
    (D) related
    (E) well-known

14. METHODICALLY
    (A) calmly
    (B) carelessly
    (C) openly
    (D) systematically
    (E) vigorously

15. LISTLESS
    (A) attentive
    (B) delighted
    (C) slender
    (D) languid
    (E) thoughtful

16. INGENIOUS
    (A) clever
    (B) crafty
    (C) insipid
    (D) naive
    (E) sincere

17. OBSTRUCT
    (A) block
    (B) build
    (C) disturb
    (D) experiment
    (E) imprison

18. HUMANE
    (A) benevolent
    (B) convincing
    (C) traditional
    (D) virile
    (E) welcome

19. EMISSARY
    (A) alien
    (B) pioneer
    (C) envoy
    (D) saboteur
    (E) substitute

20. INFESTED
    (A) devoured
    (B) introduced
    (C) overrun
    (D) surrounded
    (E) tainted

Vocabulary Test 33

1. ABRIDGE
   (A) dilate
   (B) shorten
   (C) go over
   (D) build
   (E) connect

2. HUMID
   (A) funny
   (B) hot
   (C) kindly
   (D) moist
   (E) normal

3. STABILIZE
   (A) fasten
   (B) pick
   (C) steady
   (D) succor
   (E) vary

4. PENSIVE
   (A) awkward
   (B) declining
   (C) iridescent
   (D) thoughtful
   (E) thwarted

5. ALLOT
   (A) apportion
   (B) economize
   (C) offer
   (D) permit
   (E) restrict

6. IMPEACH
   (A) accuse
   (B) convict
   (C) sear
   (D) preserve
   (E) pierce

7. PREDICAMENT
   (A) argument
   (B) danger
   (C) plight
   (D) prominence
   (E) struggle

8. INFRINGEMENT
   (A) admission
   (B) assessment
   (C) dissolution
   (D) restriction
   (E) violation

9. SANCTION
   (A) condemn
   (B) destroy
   (C) neutralize
   (D) terrify
   (E) ratify

10. VINDICTIVE
    (A) colorful
    (B) helpful
    (C) sour
    (D) revengeful
    (E) winning

11. DEADLOCK
    (A) useless material
    (B) fatigue
    (C) will
    (D) fixed limit
    (E) state of inaction

12. DEPUTY
    (A) arranger
    (B) detective
    (C) fugitive
    (D) substitute
    (E) cleanser

13. OPPRESS
    (A) conclude
    (B) crush
    (C) branch out
    (D) alter
    (E) stay within

14. REVELATION
    (A) respect
    (B) disclosure
    (C) repetition
    (D) suitability
    (E) remainder

15. IRKSOME
    (A) unreasonable
    (B) unclean
    (C) related
    (D) aglow
    (E) tedious

16. SALLOW
    (A) yellowish
    (B) external
    (C) healing
    (D) quiet
    (E) vague

17. IMPERIOUS
    (A) large
    (B) surprising
    (C) overbearing
    (D) mischievous
    (E) healthy

18. STRINGENT
    (A) rigid
    (B) threaded
    (C) musty
    (D) obtainable
    (E) avoided

19. ATTRIBUTE
    (A) characteristic
    (B) donation
    (C) friction
    (D) vengeance
    (E) dress

20. WRANGLE
    (A) dispute
    (B) come to grips
    (C) squirm
    (D) expel moisture
    (E) plead

Vocabulary Test 34

1. COMMEND
   (A) begin
   (B) praise
   (C) remark
   (D) graduate
   (E) plead

2. PLACID
   (A) public
   (B) watered
   (C) quiet
   (D) established
   (E) colorless

3. SEGREGATE
   (A) multiply
   (B) encircle
   (C) conform
   (D) isolate
   (E) deny

4. DERIDE
   (A) plead
   (B) mock
   (C) appeal
   (D) surprise
   (E) obligate

5. GUILE
   (A) blame
   (B) market
   (C) direction
   (D) deceit
   (E) throat

6. PRUDENT
   (A) critical
   (B) cautious
   (C) bluish
   (D) unfinished
   (E) outrageous

7. BRUNT
   (A) mistake
   (B) tact
   (C) swine
   (D) force
   (E) scald

8. IMPETUOUS
   (A) faultless
   (B) masterful
   (C) insolent
   (D) urgent
   (E) hasty

9. COMPUTE
   (A) reckon
   (B) shorten
   (C) concede
   (D) deny
   (E) enclose

10. SQUALID
    (A) unrealistic
    (B) crouching
    (C) filthy
    (D) fretful
    (E) flattened

11. ULTIMATUM
    (A) shrewd plan
    (B) final terms
    (C) first defeat
    (D) dominant leader
    (E) electric motor

12. GIRD
    (A) surround
    (B) appeal
    (C) request
    (D) break
    (E) glance

13. WANGLE
    (A) moan
    (B) mutilate
    (C) exasperate
    (D) manipulate
    (E) triumph

14. PROCUREMENT
    (A) acquisition
    (B) resolution
    (C) healing
    (D) importance
    (E) miracle

15. CULMINATION
    (A) rebellion
    (B) lighting system
    (C) climax
    (D) destruction
    (E) mystery

16. INSUPERABLE
    (A) incomprehensible
    (B) elaborate
    (C) unusual
    (D) indigestible
    (E) unconquerable

17. CLICHÉ
    (A) summary argument
    (B) new information
    (C) new hat
    (D) trite phrase
    (E) lock devise

18. CONCESSION
    (A) nourishment
    (B) plea
    (C) restoration
    (D) similarity
    (E) acknowledgment

19. INSIPID
    (A) disrespectful
    (B) uninteresting
    (C) persistent
    (D) whole
    (E) stimulating

20. REPRISAL
    (A) retaliation
    (B) drawing
    (C) capture
    (D) release
    (E) suspicion

Vocabulary Test 35

1. SIGNIFICANT
   (A) needless
   (B) real
   (C) childish
   (D) important
   (E) precise

2. DOGGED
   (A) obstinate
   (B) sickly
   (C) poetic
   (D) honorable
   (E) religious

3. CUSTODY
   (A) dessert
   (B) plea for action
   (C) swearing
   (D) imprisonment
   (E) regard

4. RESIDUE
   (A) remainder
   (B) evaporation
   (C) rent
   (D) admission
   (E) payment

5. MERGER
   (A) leniency
   (B) plunge
   (C) detective
   (D) magician
   (E) consolidation

6. OBSCURITY
   (A) slyness
   (B) indistinctness
   (C) ease
   (D) disappearance
   (E) sadness

7. ACCORD
   (A) opposition
   (B) agreement
   (C) praise
   (D) exclamation
   (E) helpfulness

8. RIGOR
   (A) activity
   (B) shagginess
   (C) sorrow
   (D) severity
   (E) repayment

9. RESOLUTELY
   (A) fully
   (B) briefly
   (C) firmly
   (D) finally
   (E) calmly

10. AUSTERITY
    (A) heat
    (B) displeasure
    (C) honesty
    (D) hospitableness
    (E) sternness

11. DUBIOUS
    (A) economical
    (B) well-groomed
    (C) boring
    (D) discouraged
    (E) uncertain

12. ATROCIOUS
    (A) brutal
    (B) innocent
    (C) shrunken
    (D) yellowish
    (E) unsound

13. BLITHE
    (A) wicked
    (B) criminal
    (C) merry
    (D) unintelligible
    (E) substantial

14. PRESTIGE
    (A) speed
    (B) influence
    (C) omen
    (D) pride
    (E) excuse

15. TRITE
    (A) brilliant
    (B) unusual
    (C) funny
    (D) stiff
    (E) commonplace

16. VINDICATE
    (A) outrage
    (B) waver
    (C) enliven
    (D) justify
    (E) fuse

17. EXUDE
    (A) accuse
    (B) discharge
    (C) inflect
    (D) appropriate
    (E) distress

18. LIVID
    (A) burned
    (B) patient
    (C) hurt
    (D) salted
    (E) discolored

19. FACTION
    (A) clique
    (B) judgment
    (C) truth
    (D) type of architecture
    (E) health

20. INCLEMENT
    (A) merciful
    (B) sloping
    (C) harsh
    (D) disastrous
    (E) personal

Vocabulary Test 36

1. FOIL
   (A) defeat
   (B) punish
   (C) accuse
   (D) pray
   (E) return

2. PREVALENT
   (A) brilliant
   (B) mediocre
   (C) previous
   (D) occurring often
   (E) occurring seldom

3. CONTEMPLATE
   (A) recall
   (B) consider
   (C) respect
   (D) commit
   (E) distribute

4. CRYSTALLIZE
   (A) overwhelm completely
   (B) lead to confusion
   (C) assume definite form
   (D) blame
   (E) glamorize

5. SORCERY
   (A) ancestry
   (B) grief
   (C) acidity
   (D) filth
   (E) witchcraft

6. RETROSPECT
   (A) withdrawal
   (B) review of the past
   (C) very severe punishment
   (D) prediction
   (E) self-examination

7. VENEER
   (A) respect
   (B) arrival
   (C) poison
   (D) summons
   (E) gloss

8. SUBSIDIZE
   (A) store for later use
   (B) aid with public money
   (C) place under military control
   (D) check
   (E) ridicule in public

9. OMINOUS
   (A) devouring everything
   (B) all-inclusive
   (C) having two meanings
   (D) foreboding
   (E) vegetable

10. INADVERTENTLY
    (A) actually
    (B) harmlessly
    (C) heedlessly
    (D) angrily
    (E) confidently

11. AUTHORIZE
    (A) compose
    (B) self-educate
    (C) permit
    (D) manage
    (E) complicate

12. VERSATILE
    (A) imaginative
    (B) many-sided
    (C) proud
    (D) upright
    (E) self-centered

13. OPPORTUNE
    (A) self-confident
    (B) rare
    (C) frequent
    (D) timely
    (E) contrasting

14. STIFLE
    (A) smother
    (B) yawn
    (C) heighten
    (D) promise
    (E) strike

15. ACRID
    (A) agricultural
    (B) athletic
    (C) extremely tasty
    (D) fierce
    (E) bitterly irritating

16. FUTILITY
    (A) loyalty
    (B) evil
    (C) faith
    (D) hatred
    (E) uselessness

17. METAPHOR
    (A) unrhymed poetry
    (B) change of structure
    (C) part of a foot
    (D) implied comparison
    (E) signal light

18. STATIC
    (A) not moving
    (B) referring to the state
    (C) itemized
    (D) clear
    (E) pointed

19. TENTATIVE
    (A) formal
    (B) experimental
    (C) affectionate
    (D) tight
    (E) progressive

20. FORESTALL
    (A) dispossess
    (B) overshadow
    (C) anticipate
    (D) establish
    (E) prepare

Vocabulary Test 37

1. SULK
   (A) cry
   (B) annoy
   (C) lament
   (D) be sullen
   (E) scorn

2. FLOUNDER
   (A) investigate
   (B) label
   (C) struggle
   (D) consent
   (E) escape

3. PARLEY
   (A) discussion
   (B) thoroughfare
   (C) salon
   (D) surrender
   (E) division

4. MAESTRO
   (A) official
   (B) ancestor
   (C) teacher
   (D) watchman
   (E) alien

5. MEANDERING
   (A) cruel
   (B) adjusting
   (C) winding
   (D) smooth
   (E) combining

6. GNARLED
   (A) angry
   (B) bitter
   (C) twisted
   (D) ancient
   (E) embroidered

7. TEMPERANCE
   (A) moderation
   (B) climate
   (C) carelessness
   (D) disagreeableness
   (E) rigidity

8. PRECARIOUS
   (A) foresighted
   (B) careful
   (C) modest
   (D) headstrong
   (E) uncertain

9. COVETOUS
   (A) undisciplined
   (B) grasping
   (C) timid
   (D) insincere
   (E) secretive

10. PRIVATION
    (A) reward
    (B) superiority in rank
    (C) hardship
    (D) suitability of behavior
    (E) solitude

11. DESIGNATE
    (A) draw
    (B) expel
    (C) permit
    (D) name
    (E) repeat

12. BIPARTISAN
    (A) adhering to views of one
        party
    (B) prejudiced
    (C) representing two parties
    (D) bisected
    (E) narrow

13. FERVOR
    (A) artistic ability
    (B) hatred
    (C) kindness
    (D) intense feeling
    (E) coldness

14. ELUSIVE
    (A) helpful
    (B) baffling
    (C) abundant
    (D) lessening
    (E) expanding

15. EXPLOIT
    (A) utilize
    (B) favor
    (C) expel
    (D) pool
    (E) labor

16. ANECDOTE
    (A) equipment
    (B) remedy for poison
    (C) brief narrative
    (D) inquiry
    (E) hysteria

17. USURP
    (A) seize by force
    (B) accompany
    (C) become useful
    (D) move cityward
    (E) return

18. WILY
    (A) stubborn
    (B) graceful
    (C) nervous
    (D) insignificant
    (E) crafty

19. NOMENCLATURE
    (A) election
    (B) system of names
    (C) morality
    (D) grammar
    (E) migration

20. ACQUIESCE
    (A) provide
    (B) share
    (C) climb
    (D) submit
    (E) proceed

Vocabulary Test 38

1. CRUCIAL
   (A) technical
   (B) decisive
   (C) ill-natured
   (D) inelegant
   (E) greatly distorted

2. IMPLICATE
   (A) please
   (B) expect
   (C) involve
   (D) trick
   (E) ambush

3. DOMESTIC
   (A) internal
   (B) alien
   (C) untrained
   (D) political
   (E) beneficial

4. AUDACIOUS
   (A) daring
   (B) fearful
   (C) indifferent
   (D) attentive
   (E) wicked

5. BUOYANT
   (A) unwise
   (B) cheerful
   (C) alarming
   (D) uncertain
   (E) juvenile

6. GAUNT
   (A) stiff
   (B) white
   (C) repulsive
   (D) harsh-sounding
   (E) lean

7. PHOBIA
   (A) temper
   (B) disease
   (C) puzzle
   (D) dream
   (E) fear

8. DIVERSITY
   (A) amusement
   (B) discouragement
   (C) variety
   (D) mistrust
   (E) confusion

9. PRESUMPTUOUS
   (A) forward
   (B) foreshadowing
   (C) costly
   (D) renewable
   (E) unhealthful

10. ENIGMATIC
    (A) sarcastic
    (B) skillful
    (C) puzzling
    (D) healthy
    (E) like an insect

11. INFILTRATE
    (A) pass through
    (B) stop
    (C) consider
    (D) challenge openly
    (E) meet secretly

12. REVOCATION
    (A) certificate
    (B) repeal
    (C) animation
    (D) license
    (E) pleas

13. LOQUACIOUS
    (A) grim
    (B) stern
    (C) talkative
    (D) light-hearted
    (E) liberty-loving

14. APERTURE
    (A) basement
    (B) opening
    (C) phantom
    (D) protective coloring
    (E) light refreshment

15. PUNGENT
    (A) biting
    (B) smooth
    (C) quarrelsome
    (D) wrong
    (E) proud

16. CORROBORATE
    (A) deny
    (B) elaborate
    (C) confirm
    (D) gnaw
    (E) state

17. BENEVOLENCE
    (A) good fortune
    (B) well-being
    (C) inheritance
    (D) violence
    (E) charitableness

18. PETULANT
    (A) rotten
    (B) fretful
    (C) unrelated
    (D) weird
    (E) throbbing

19. DERELICT
    (A) abandoned
    (B) widowed
    (C) faithful
    (D) insincere
    (E) hysterical

20. INCISIVE
    (A) stimulating
    (B) accidental
    (C) brief
    (D) penetrating
    (E) final

Vocabulary Test 39

1. DWINDLE
   (A) hang loosely
   (B) decisive
   (C) fight
   (D) share
   (E) decrease

2. FORTHRIGHT
   (A) direct
   (B) constitutional
   (C) unpleasant
   (D) polite
   (E) accidental

3. VIGILANT
   (A) forceful
   (B) immoral
   (C) alert
   (D) sightless
   (E) many-sided

4. CONFIRMATION
   (A) trust
   (B) suspense
   (C) encounter
   (D) restraint
   (E) proof

5. PREVAIL
   (A) introduce
   (B) misjudge
   (C) rescue
   (D) triumph
   (E) overestimate

6. ALOOF
   (A) hard
   (B) imaginary
   (C) reserved
   (D) happy
   (E) willing

7. UNSCRUPULOUS
   (A) unprincipled
   (B) unbalanced
   (C) careless
   (D) disfigured
   (E) obstinate

8. PROFOUND
   (A) deep
   (B) disrespectful
   (C) plentiful
   (D) positive
   (E) expert

9. PRETEXT
   (A) argument
   (B) excuse
   (C) preliminary examination
   (D) first glimpse
   (E) sermon

10. INFER
    (A) surprise
    (B) hope
    (C) disagree
    (D) conclude
    (E) shift quickly

11. LAUD
    (A) praise
    (B) cleanse
    (C) replace
    (D) squander
    (E) frown upon

12. TAUNT
    (A) jeer at
    (B) tighten
    (C) rescue
    (D) interest
    (E) ward off

13. DEITY
    (A) renown
    (B) divinity
    (C) delicacy
    (D) destiny
    (E) futility

14. GRAVITY
    (A) displeasure
    (B) thankfulness
    (C) suffering
    (D) roughness
    (E) seriousness

15. CONTEMPTUOUS
    (A) thoughtful
    (B) soiled
    (C) dishonorable
    (D) scornful
    (E) self-satisfied

16. WAIVE
    (A) exercise
    (B) swing
    (C) claim
    (D) give up
    (E) wear out

17. ASPIRE
    (A) fade away
    (B) excite
    (C) desire earnestly
    (D) breathe heavily
    (E) roughen

18. PERTINENT
    (A) related
    (B) saucy
    (C) quick
    (D) impatient
    (E) excited

19. DEVASTATION
    (A) desolation
    (B) displeasure
    (C) dishonor
    (D) neglect
    (E) religious fervor

20. IMMINENT
    (A) sudden
    (B) important
    (C) delayed
    (D) threatening
    (E) forceful

Vocabulary Test 40

1. CONTROVERSIAL
   (A) faultfinding
   (B) pleasant
   (C) debatable
   (D) ugly
   (E) talkative

2. GHASTLY
   (A) hasty
   (B) furious
   (C) breathless
   (D) deathlike
   (E) spiritual

3. BELLIGERENT
   (A) worldly
   (B) warlike
   (C) loudmouthed
   (D) furious
   (E) artistic

4. PROFICIENCY
   (A) wisdom
   (B) oversupply
   (C) expertness
   (D) advancement
   (E) sincerity

5. COMPASSION
   (A) rage
   (B) strength of character
   (C) forcefulness
   (D) sympathy
   (E) uniformity

6. DISSENSION
   (A) treatise
   (B) pretense
   (C) fear
   (D) lineage
   (E) discord

7. INTIMATE
   (A) charm
   (B) hint
   (C) disguise
   (D) frighten
   (E) hum

8. BERATE
   (A) classify
   (B) scold
   (C) underestimate
   (D) take one's time
   (E) evaluate

9. DEARTH
   (A) scarcity
   (B) width
   (C) affection
   (D) wealth
   (E) warmth

10. MEDITATE
    (A) rest
    (B) stare
    (C) doze
    (D) make peace
    (E) reflect

11. BONDAGE
    (A) poverty
    (B) redemption
    (C) slavery
    (D) retirement
    (E) complaint

12. AGILITY
    (A) wisdom
    (B) nimbleness
    (C) agreeableness
    (D) simplicity
    (E) excitement

13. ABDICATE
    (A) achieve
    (B) protest
    (C) renounce
    (D) demand
    (E) steal

14. STIFLE
    (A) talk nonsense
    (B) sidestep
    (C) depress
    (D) smother
    (E) stick

15. EDICT
    (A) abbreviation
    (B) lie
    (C) carbon copy
    (D) correction
    (E) decree

16. AMITY
    (A) ill will
    (B) hope
    (C) pity
    (D) friendship
    (E) pleasure

17. COERCION
    (A) force
    (B) disgust
    (C) suspicion
    (D) pleasure
    (E) criticism

18. ABASH
    (A) embarrass
    (B) encourage
    (C) punish
    (D) surrender
    (E) overthrow

19. TACITURN
    (A) weak
    (B) evil
    (C) tender
    (D) silent
    (E) sensitive

20. REMISS
    (A) memorable
    (B) neglectful
    (C) useless
    (D) prompt
    (E) exact

Vocabulary Test 41

1. IMMORTAL
   (A) disgraceful
   (B) stupendous
   (C) steadfast
   (D) blameless
   (E) imperishable

2. CRAFTY
   (A) sly
   (B) irritable
   (C) seaworthy
   (D) operatic
   (E) municipal

3. QUIRK
   (A) opportunity
   (B) questioning
   (C) peculiarity
   (D) mistaken identity
   (E) persistent annoyance

4. ADEPT
   (A) grateful
   (B) additional
   (C) awkward
   (D) skillful
   (E) orderly

5. DISSUADE
   (A) discharge
   (B) discourage
   (C) underrate
   (D) convince
   (E) lead astray

6. RECIPROCAL
   (A) independent
   (B) remorseful
   (C) commercial
   (D) international
   (E) mutual

7. VOGUE
   (A) picture
   (B) history
   (C) cloudiness
   (D) popularity
   (E) mischief

8. FLAIR
   (A) aptitude
   (B) bright light
   (C) anger
   (D) boasting remark
   (E) frightening experience

9. COVET
   (A) shelter
   (B) crave
   (C) crouch
   (D) bargain
   (E) hatch

10. LANGUID
    (A) roundabout
    (B) learned
    (C) spiritless
    (D) hidden
    (E) praiseworthy

11. ARID
    (A) mountainous
    (B) fragrant
    (C) soiled
    (D) dry
    (E) productive

12. DEFRAUD
    (A) cheat
    (B) uncover
    (C) pay
    (D) delay
    (E) accuse

13. DELUGE
    (A) deceive
    (B) follow
    (C) conclude
    (D) transport
    (E) overwhelm

14. POMPOUS
    (A) occasionally leaky
    (B) self-important
    (C) thoughtful
    (D) powerful
    (E) respectful

15. HARASS
    (A) rave
    (B) shelter
    (C) pierce
    (D) restrain
    (E) torment

16. APPARITION
    (A) skeleton
    (B) fort
    (C) ghost
    (D) dream
    (E) insect

17. INFAMOUS
    (A) detestable
    (B) humble
    (C) gloomy
    (D) scholarly
    (E) unsuspected

18. CHRONIC
    (A) irritable
    (B) historic
    (C) sudden
    (D) habitual
    (E) timely

19. TERSELY
    (A) vigorously
    (B) with difficulty
    (C) informally
    (D) physically
    (E) concisely

20. IMPERTURBABLE
    (A) quick-tempered
    (B) calm
    (C) envious
    (D) excitable
    (E) impassable

Vocabulary Test 42

1. STAGNANT
   (A) inactive
   (B) alert
   (C) selfish
   (D) difficult
   (E) scornful

2. MANDATORY
   (A) insane
   (B) obligatory
   (C) evident
   (D) strategic
   (E) unequaled

3. INFERNAL
   (A) immodest
   (B) incomplete
   (C) domestic
   (D) second-rate
   (E) fiendish

4. EXONERATE
   (A) free from blame
   (B) warn
   (C) drive out
   (D) overcharge
   (E) plead

5. ARBITER
   (A) friend
   (B) judge
   (C) drug
   (D) tree surgeon
   (E) truant

6. ENMITY
   (A) boredom
   (B) puzzle
   (C) offensive language
   (D) ill will
   (E) entanglement

7. DISCRIMINATE
   (A) fail
   (B) delay
   (C) accuse
   (D) distinguish
   (E) reject

8. DERISION
   (A) disgust
   (B) ridicule
   (C) fear
   (D) anger
   (E) heredity

9. EXULTANT
   (A) essential
   (B) elated
   (C) praiseworthy
   (D) plentiful
   (E) high-priced

10. OSTENSIBLE
    (A) vibrating
    (B) odd
    (C) apparent
    (D) standard
    (E) ornate

11. CURTAIL
    (A) jump
    (B) lessen
    (C) design
    (D) collect
    (E) dance

12. INVERSE
    (A) opposite
    (B) immovable
    (C) remote
    (D) progressive
    (E) complicated

13. SUAVE
    (A) careful
    (B) attractive
    (C) foreign
    (D) unnatural
    (E) polished

14. FEASIBLE
    (A) indefinite
    (B) practicable
    (C) inadvisable
    (D) edible
    (E) prominent

15. ANIMATE
    (A) paint
    (B) praise highly
    (C) enliven
    (D) suggest indirectly
    (E) debate

16. STRIFE
    (A) conflict
    (B) weariness
    (C) joy
    (D) union
    (E) strength

17. AVOWAL
    (A) vacancy
    (B) hobby
    (C) desertion
    (D) settled dislike
    (E) open declaration

18. REBUFF
    (A) deduct
    (B) cancel
    (C) snub
    (D) return
    (E) echo

19. REPUDIATE
    (A) hail
    (B) support
    (C) start
    (D) disown
    (E) duplicate

20. WILY
    (A) graceful
    (B) drooping
    (C) cunning
    (D) untamed
    (E) nervous

Vocabulary Test 43

1. FIDELITY
   (A) selfishness
   (B) faithfulness
   (C) cruelty
   (D) indifference
   (E) weakness

2. AVERT
   (A) prevent
   (B) convince
   (C) flee
   (D) meet
   (E) fear

3. TEPID
   (A) hesitant
   (B) fierce
   (C) lukewarm
   (D) singular
   (E) temperamental

4. EXCERPT
   (A) omission
   (B) sales tax
   (C) cancellation
   (D) pleasure trip
   (E) selected passage

5. INTERMINABLE
   (A) periodic
   (B) unbearable
   (C) well-blended
   (D) short-lived
   (E) unending

6. PRECIPICE
   (A) forecast
   (B) cliff
   (C) danger
   (D) instructor
   (E) obstinacy

7. SCRUTINY
   (A) muscle
   (B) advertising
   (C) scowl
   (D) close examination
   (E) tense situation

8. REPUGNANT
   (A) distasteful
   (B) irritable
   (C) regretful
   (D) honored
   (E) restful

9. ALLOCATE
   (A) address
   (B) tempt
   (C) distribute
   (D) permit
   (E) drift

10. PROFUSION
    (A) declaration
    (B) abundance
    (C) skillfulness
    (D) depth
    (E) anxiety

11. ABHOR
    (A) hate
    (B) admire
    (C) taste
    (D) skip
    (E) resign

12. DUTIFUL
    (A) lasting
    (B) sluggish
    (C) required
    (D) soothing
    (E) obedient

13. ZEALOT
    (A) breeze
    (B) enthusiast
    (C) vault
    (D) wild animal
    (E) musical instrument

14. MAGNANIMOUS
    (A) high-minded
    (B) faithful
    (C) concerned
    (D) individual
    (E) small

15. CITE
    (A) protest
    (B) depart
    (C) quote
    (D) agitate
    (E) perform

16. OBLIVION
    (A) hindrance
    (B) accident
    (C) courtesy
    (D) forgetfulness
    (E) old age

17. CARDINAL
    (A) independent
    (B) well-organized
    (C) subordinate
    (D) dignified
    (E) chief

18. DEPLETE
    (A) restrain
    (B) corrupt
    (C) despair
    (D) exhaust
    (E) spread out

19. SUPERSEDE
    (A) retire
    (B) replace
    (C) overflow
    (D) bless
    (E) oversee

20. SPORADIC
    (A) bad-tempered
    (B) infrequent
    (C) radical
    (D) reckless
    (E) humble

Vocabulary Test 44

1. NEUTRALIZE
   (A) entangle
   (B) strengthen
   (C) counteract
   (D) combat
   (E) converse

2. INSINUATE
   (A) destroy
   (B) hint
   (C) do wrong
   (D) accuse
   (E) release

3. DIMINUTIVE
   (A) proud
   (B) slow
   (C) small
   (D) watery
   (E) puzzling

4. PLIGHT
   (A) departure
   (B) weight
   (C) conspiracy
   (D) predicament
   (E) stamp

5. ILLICIT
   (A) unlawful
   (B) overpowering
   (C) ill-advised
   (D) small-scale
   (E) unreadable

6. BENIGN
   (A) contagious
   (B) fatal
   (C) ignorant
   (D) kindly
   (E) decorative

7. REVERIE
   (A) abusive language
   (B) love song
   (C) backward step
   (D) daydream
   (E) holy man

8. APPREHENSIVE
   (A) quiet
   (B) firm
   (C) curious
   (D) sincere
   (E) fearful

9. RECOIL
   (A) shrink
   (B) attract
   (C) electrify
   (D) adjust
   (E) enroll

10. GUISE
    (A) trickery
    (B) request
    (C) innocence
    (D) misdeed
    (E) appearance

11. FLUCTUATE
   (A) fall
   (B) impede
   (C) waver
   (D) raise
   (E) hasten

12. TRANQUIL
   (A) restless
   (B) calm
   (C) weary
   (D) understanding
   (E) blooming

13. STALEMATE
   (A) deadlock
   (B) excuse
   (C) panic
   (D) boredom
   (E) contract

14. IRRELEVANT
   (A) disrespectful
   (B) tolerant
   (C) sinful
   (D) unrelated
   (E) unresponsive

15. AUXILIARY
   (A) greedy
   (B) well-proportioned
   (C) self-governing
   (D) military
   (E) assistant

16. PROCRASTINATE
   (A) tell a lie
   (B) dismiss
   (C) postpone
   (D) furnish
   (E) imitate

17. FACILE
   (A) extraordinary
   (B) queer
   (C) breakable
   (D) easy
   (E) impossible

18. OBESE
   (A) lawful
   (B) extremely fat
   (C) challenging
   (D) bowing deeply
   (E) sad-faced

19. AUGMENT
   (A) increase
   (B) predict
   (C) disclose
   (D) challenge
   (E) testify

20. RESPITE
   (A) feud
   (B) receipt
   (C) flattery
   (D) teasing
   (E) lull

Vocabulary Test 45

1. INTRICATE
   (A) thin
   (B) reliable
   (C) sly
   (D) safe from danger
   (E) complicated

2. INTEGRITY
   (A) honesty
   (B) interest
   (C) comfort
   (D) width
   (E) pride

3. DISPEL
   (A) rush
   (B) alarm
   (C) scatter
   (D) amuse
   (E) bewitch

4. PSEUDONYM
   (A) title of nobility
   (B) lack of a name
   (C) family name
   (D) pen name
   (E) dishonorable name

5. SURMOUNT
   (A) conquer
   (B) release
   (C) escape
   (D) inset
   (E) display

6. DIRE
   (A) grimy
   (B) noisy
   (C) stubborn
   (D) dreadful
   (E) sharp-edged

7. INCOHERENT
   (A) irritable
   (B) uncomfortable
   (C) disconnected
   (D) unequaled
   (E) ineffective

8. ABOUND
   (A) jump about
   (B) be plentiful
   (C) shorten
   (D) forsake
   (E) limit

9. BESTOW
   (A) discolor
   (B) invade
   (C) confer
   (D) decorate
   (E) occur

10. RUDIMENTARY
    (A) web-like
    (B) elementary
    (C) systematic
    (D) structural
    (E) discourteous

11. RELINQUISH
    (A) regret
    (B) abandon
    (C) pursue
    (D) secure
    (E) penetrate

12. INJUNCTION
    (A) error
    (B) attack
    (C) injustice
    (D) suggestion
    (E) order

13. ADVENT
    (A) attachment
    (B) reference
    (C) arrival
    (D) excitement
    (E) complaint

14. BICAMERAL
    (A) dealing with life forms
    (B) meeting on alternate years
    (C) over-sweet
    (D) having two legislative
        branches
    (E) having two meanings

15. PERVERSE
    (A) contrary
    (B) stingy
    (C) unfortunate
    (D) hereditary
    (E) easygoing

16. THWART
    (A) assist
    (B) whimper
    (C) slice
    (D) escape
    (E) block

17. DEVOID
    (A) empty
    (B) illegal
    (C) affectionate
    (D) pious
    (E) annoying

18. BLAND
    (A) gentle
    (B) guilty
    (C) salty
    (D) unfinished
    (E) majestic

19. OSTRACIZE
    (A) flatter
    (B) scold
    (C) show off
    (D) banish
    (E) vibrate

20. CANDOR
    (A) sociability
    (B) outspokenness
    (C) grief
    (D) light
    (E) flattery

Vocabulary Test 46

1. ACQUIT
   (A) increase
   (B) harden
   (C) clear
   (D) sharpen
   (E) sentence

2. DEXTERITY
   (A) conceit
   (B) skill
   (C) insistence
   (D) embarrassment
   (E) guidance

3. ASSIMILATE
   (A) absorb
   (B) imitate
   (C) maintain
   (D) outrun
   (E) curb

4. DESPONDENCY
   (A) relief
   (B) gratitude
   (C) dejection
   (D) hatred
   (E) poverty

5. BUOYANT
   (A) conceited
   (B) cautioning
   (C) youthful
   (D) musical
   (E) cheerful

6. CULINARY
   (A) having to do with cooking
   (B) pertaining to dressmaking
   (C) fond of eating
   (D) loving money
   (E) tending to be secretive

7. CAPRICE
   (A) wisdom
   (B) ornament
   (C) pillar
   (D) whim
   (E) energy

8. DETERRENT
   (A) restraining
   (B) cleansing
   (C) deciding
   (D) concluding
   (E) crumbling

9. PUGNACIOUS
   (A) sticky
   (B) cowardly
   (C) precise
   (D) vigorous
   (E) quarrelsome

10. ABSCOND
    (A) detest
    (B) reduce
    (C) swallow up
    (D) dismiss
    (E) flee

11. BOUNTY
    (A) limit
    (B) boastfulness
    (C) cheerfulness
    (D) reward
    (E) punishment

12. NOVICE
    (A) storyteller
    (B) iceberg
    (C) adolescent
    (D) mythical creature
    (E) beginning

13. BOLSTER
    (A) contradict
    (B) insist
    (C) defy
    (D) sleep
    (E) prop

14. MOBILE
    (A) changeable
    (B) scornful
    (C) mechanical
    (D) stylish
    (E) solid

15. CREDULITY
    (A) prize
    (B) feebleness
    (C) balance
    (D) laziness
    (E) belief

16. DOLDRUMS
    (A) charity
    (B) curing agents
    (C) contagious disease
    (D) low spirits
    (E) places of safety

17. LOATH
    (A) idle
    (B) worried
    (C) unwilling
    (D) ready
    (E) sad

18. ADROIT
    (A) aimless
    (B) clever
    (C) moist
    (D) false
    (E) nearby

19. LITHE
    (A) tough
    (B) obstinate
    (C) flexible
    (D) damp
    (E) gay

20. VACILLATE
    (A) waver
    (B) defeat
    (C) favor
    (D) endanger
    (E) humiliate

Vocabulary Test 47

1. PREVARICATE
   (A) hesitate
   (B) lie
   (C) protest
   (D) ramble
   (E) remain silent

2. INCREDULOUS
   (A) argumentative
   (B) imaginative
   (C) indifferent
   (D) irreligious
   (E) skeptical

3. PLACATE
   (A) amuse
   (B) appease
   (C) embroil
   (D) pity
   (E) reject

4. COGNIZANT
   (A) afraid
   (B) aware
   (C) capable
   (D) ignorant
   (E) optimistic

5. DISSONANCE
   (A) disapproval
   (B) disaster
   (C) discord
   (D) disparity
   (E) dissimilarity

6. IMMINENT
   (A) declining
   (B) distinguished
   (C) impending
   (D) terrifying
   (E) unlikely

7. TORSION
   (A) bending
   (B) compressing
   (C) sliding
   (D) stretching
   (E) twisting

8. ACCRUED
   (A) added
   (B) incidental
   (C) miscellaneous
   (D) special
   (E) unearned

9. EFFRONTERY
   (A) bad taste
   (B) conceit
   (C) dishonesty
   (D) imprudence
   (E) snobbishness

10. ACQUIESCENCE
    (A) advice
    (B) advocacy
    (C) compliance
    (D) friendliness
    (E) opposition

11. RETICENT
(A) fidgety
(B) repetitious
(C) reserved
(D) restful
(E) truthful

12. STIPULATE
(A) bargain
(B) instigate
(C) prefer
(D) request
(E) specify

13. PSEUDO
(A) deep
(B) obvious
(C) pretend
(D) provoking
(E) spiritual

14. FLOTSAM
(A) dark sand
(B) fleet
(C) life preserver
(D) shoreline
(E) wreckage

15. AWRY
(A) askew
(B) deplorable
(C) odd
(D) simple
(E) striking

16. NEFARIOUS
(A) clever
(B) necessary
(C) negligent
(D) shortsighted
(E) wicked

17. GLIB
(A) cheerful
(B) delightful
(C) dull
(D) fluent
(E) gloomy

18. PAUCITY
(A) abundance
(B) ease
(C) hardship
(D) lack
(E) stoppage

19. LUCRATIVE
(A) debasing
(B) fortunate
(C) influential
(D) monetary
(E) profitable

20. INDUBITABLE
(A) doubtful
(B) fraudulent
(C) honorable
(D) safe
(E) undeniable

Vocabulary Test 48

1. CONNIVANCE
   (A) approval
   (B) collusion
   (C) conflict
   (D) permission
   (E) theft

2. SAVANT
   (A) diplomat
   (B) inventor
   (C) learned man
   (D) thrifty person
   (E) wiseacre

3. INCIPIENT
   (A) beginning
   (B) dangerous
   (C) hasty
   (D) secret
   (E) widespread

4. VIRILE
   (A) honest
   (B) loyal
   (C) manly
   (D) pugnacious
   (E) virtuous

5. ASSIDUOUS
   (A) courteous
   (B) diligent
   (C) discouraged
   (D) frank
   (E) slow

6. CATACLYSM
   (A) blunder
   (B) superstition
   (C) treachery
   (D) triumph
   (E) upheaval

7. AUSPICIOUS
   (A) condemnatory
   (B) conspicuous
   (C) favorable
   (D) questionable
   (E) spicy

8. BANTER
   (A) conversation
   (B) criticism
   (C) gossip
   (D) irony
   (E) jesting

9. VERNACULAR
   (A) common speech
   (B) correct usage
   (C) long words
   (D) oratory
   (E) poetic style

10. EMOLUMENT
    (A) capital
    (B) compensation
    (C) liabilities
    (D) loss
    (E) output

11. TURGID
    (A) dusty
    (B) muddy
    (C) rolling
    (D) swollen
    (E) tense

12. EXPUNGE
    (A) clarify
    (B) copy
    (C) delete
    (D) investigate
    (E) underline

13. ETHNOLOGY
    (A) causation
    (B) morals
    (C) social psychology
    (D) study of races
    (E) word analysis

14. DEDUCE
    (A) diminish
    (B) infer
    (C) outline
    (D) persuade
    (E) subtract

15. PANORAMIC
    (A) brilliant
    (B) comprehensive
    (C) pretty
    (D) fluorescent
    (E) unique

16. IGNOMINY
    (A) disgrace
    (B) isolation
    (C) misfortune
    (D) sorrow
    (E) stupidity

17. RELEVANT
    (A) ingenious
    (B) inspiring
    (C) obvious
    (D) pertinent
    (E) tentative

18. GAMUT
    (A) game
    (B) range
    (C) risk
    (D) organization
    (E) plan

19. APPOSITE
    (A) appropriate
    (B) contrary
    (C) different
    (D) spontaneous
    (E) tricky

20. AMBULATORY
    (A) able to walk
    (B) confined to bed
    (C) injured
    (D) quarantined
    (E) suffering from disease

Vocabulary Test 49

1. DISPARAGE
   (A) belittle
   (B) degrade
   (C) erase
   (D) reform
   (E) scatter

2. LIMPID
   (A) calm
   (B) clear
   (C) crippled
   (D) delightful
   (E) opaque

3. DERISIVE
   (A) dividing
   (B) furnishing
   (C) reflecting
   (D) expressing ridicule
   (E) suggesting

4. DEBILITATE
   (A) encourage
   (B) insinuate
   (C) prepare
   (D) turn away
   (E) weaken

5. OPULENT
   (A) fearful
   (B) free
   (C) oversized
   (D) trustful
   (E) wealthy

6. BLANDISHMENT
   (A) dislike
   (B) flattery
   (C) ostentation
   (D) praise
   (E) rejection

7. CRYPTIC
   (A) appealing
   (B) arched
   (C) deathly
   (D) hidden
   (E) intricate

8. RAUCOUS
   (A) harsh
   (B) loud
   (C) querulous
   (D) rational
   (E) violent

9. AVIDITY
   (A) friendliness
   (B) greediness
   (C) resentment
   (D) speed
   (E) thirst

10. EPITOME
    (A) conclusion
    (B) effort
    (C) letter
    (D) summary
    (E) summit

11. HIATUS
    (A) branch
    (B) disease
    (C) gaiety
    (D) insect
    (E) opening

12. PLENARY
    (A) easy
    (B) empty
    (C) full
    (D) rewarding
    (E) untrustworthy

13. CAPRICIOUS
    (A) active
    (B) fickle
    (C) opposed
    (D) sheeplike
    (E) slippery

14. SPECIOUS
    (A) frank
    (B) particular
    (C) plausible
    (D) suspicious
    (E) vigorous

15. EXTIRPATE
    (A) besmirch
    (B) clean
    (C) eradicate
    (D) favor
    (E) subdivide

16. EQUIVOCAL
    (A) doubtful
    (B) medium
    (C) monotonous
    (D) musical
    (E) well-balanced

17. BENISON
    (A) approval
    (B) blessing
    (C) gift
    (D) prayer
    (E) reward

18. BEATIFIC
    (A) giving bliss
    (B) eager
    (C) hesitant
    (D) lovely
    (E) sad

19. SANGUINE
    (A) limp
    (B) mechanical
    (C) muddy
    (D) red
    (E) stealthy

20. SURCEASE
    (A) end
    (B) hope
    (C) resignation
    (D) sleep
    (E) sweetness

Vocabulary Test 50

1. SENTIENT
   (A) very emotional
   (B) capable of feeling
   (C) hostile
   (D) sympathetic
   (E) wise

2. OBVIATE
   (A) grasp
   (B) reform
   (C) simplify
   (D) smooth
   (E) make unnecessary

3. PERUSE
   (A) endure
   (B) perpetuate
   (C) read
   (D) undertake
   (E) urge

4. RANCOR
   (A) dignity
   (B) fierceness
   (C) odor
   (D) spite
   (E) suspicion

5. TRUNCHEON
   (A) baton
   (B) canopy
   (C) dish
   (D) gun
   (E) rejected food

6. SEBACEOUS
   (A) fatty
   (B) fluid
   (C) porous
   (D) transparent
   (E) watery

7. DILATORY
   (A) hairy
   (B) happy-go-lucky
   (C) ruined
   (D) tardy
   (E) well-to-do

8. EBULLITION
   (A) bathing
   (B) boiling
   (C) refilling
   (D) retiring
   (E) returning

9. RELEGATE
   (A) banish
   (B) deprive
   (C) designate
   (D) report
   (E) request

10. RECONDITE
   (A) brittle
   (B) concealed
   (C) explored
   (D) exposed
   (E) uninformed

11. REDOLENT
    (A) odorous
    (B) quick
    (C) refined
    (D) repulsive
    (E) supple

12. DISSIMULATE
    (A) confound
    (B) pretend
    (C) question
    (D) separate
    (E) strain

13. SUBLIME
    (A) below par
    (B) highly praised
    (C) extreme
    (D) noble
    (E) settled

14. TERMAGANT
    (A) fervor
    (B) noisy woman
    (C) sea bird
    (D) sedative
    (E) squirrel

15. SEDULOUS
    (A) deceptive
    (B) diligent
    (C) grassy
    (D) hateful
    (E) sweet

16. VITIATE
    (A) contaminate
    (B) flavor
    (C) freshen
    (D) illuminate
    (E) refer

17. CURVET
    (A) come around
    (B) follow
    (C) leap
    (D) restrain
    (E) warp

18. ADVENTITIOUS
    (A) accidental
    (B) courageous
    (C) favorable
    (D) risk taking
    (E) unexpected

19. ANIMUS
    (A) animosity
    (B) breath
    (C) faith
    (D) light
    (E) poison

20. DESCRIED
    (A) hailed
    (B) rebuffed
    (C) recalled
    (D) regretted
    (E) sighted

Answers to Vocabulary Tests

Test 1	Test 2	Test 3	Test 4
1. E	1. A	1. E	1. B
2. A	2. E	2. A	2. E
3. D	3. C	3. E	3. C
4. C	4. B	4. B	4. D
5. B	5. A	5. D	5. C
6. B	6. C	6. C	6. A
7. A	7. D	7. D	7. A
8. E	8. D	8. D	8. D
9. C	9. A	9. B	9. C
10. D	10. D	10. A	10. D
11. A	11. A	11. C	11. C
12. D	12. E	12. E	12. E
13. E	13. B	13. A	13. A
14. D	14. E	14. E	14. B
15. C	15. D	15. B	15. B
16. D	16. B	16. B	16. E
17. B	17. E	17. A	17. C
18. D	18. A	18. E	18. A
19. A	19. E	19. D	19. B
20. E	20. C	20. A	20. E

Test 5

1. B
2. E
3. B
4. B
5. B
6. E
7. C
8. D
9. A
10. C
11. A
12. A
13. D
14. D
15. E
16. C
17. D
18. B
19. C
20. B

Test 6

1. A
2. B
3. D
4. C
5. E
6. C
7. E
8. D
9. C
10. A
11. C
12. B
13. A
14. E
15. D
16. B
17. D
18. C
19. A
20. E

Test 7

1. E
2. A
3. D
4. C
5. E
6. B
7. B
8. E
9. D
10. A
11. C
12. C
13. D
14. D
15. A
16. E
17. D
18. E
19. C
20. D

Test 8

1. B
2. D
3. C
4. D
5. B
6. E
7. D
8. B
9. A
10. E
11. A
12. B
13. E
14. C
15. E
16. A
17. A
18. D
19. E
20. A

Test 9

1. B
2. C
3. E
4. B
5. E
6. A
7. D
8. D
9. B
10. E
11. B
12. C
13. A
14. C
15. D
16. C
17. B
18. D
19. D
20. C

Test 10

1. B
2. E
3. A
4. C
5. C
6. D
7. D
8. A
9. E
10. C
11. B
12. B
13. A
14. A
15. B
16. E
17. A
18. A
19. E
20. C

Test 11

1. D
2. D
3. C
4. B
5. A
6. D
7. B
8. B
9. B
10. A
11. E
12. E
13. D
14. E
15. B
16. C
17. E
18. D
19. C
20. B

Test 12

1. B
2. E
3. A
4. B
5. C
6. C
7. B
8. E
9. A
10. A
11. D
12. B
13. D
14. D
15. E
16. E
17. B
18. E
19. C
20. D

Test 13

1. C
2. D
3. E
4. C
5. C
6. C
7. B
8. E
9. E
10. C
11. A
12. A
13. D
14. D
15. A
16. E
17. A
18. D
19. D
20. B

Test 14

1. C
2. B
3. D
4. A
5. C
6. E
7. D
8. E
9. A
10. C
11. D
12. B
13. B
14. B
15. C
16. B
17. B
18. E
19. A
20. B

Test 15

1. E
2. C
3. B
4. A
5. B
6. A
7. C
8. C
9. D
10. A
11. D
12. D
13. D
14. E
15. E
16. D
17. A
18. D
19. E
20. A

Test 16

1. B
2. A
3. E
4. D
5. C
6. D
7. C
8. E
9. D
10. A
11. B
12. A
13. E
14. E
15. B
16. C
17. A
18. C
19. A
20. D

Test 17	Test 18	Test 19	Test 20
1. A	1. B	1. B	1. B
2. B	2. D	2. D	2. B
3. C	3. B	3. C	3. C
4. E	4. D	4. E	4. E
5. B	5. A	5. A	5. E
6. B	6. B	6. A	6. B
7. E	7. D	7. D	7. C
8. D	8. C	8. E	8. C
9. C	9. D	9. C	9. A
10. C	10. B	10. B	10. D
11. D	11. A	11. E	11. D
12. A	12. D	12. A	12. A
13. A	13. E	13. E	13. E
14. D	14. D	14. B	14. A
15. A	15. B	15. D	15. E
16. D	16. C	16. B	16. B
17. C	17. A	17. E	17. E
18. E	18. D	18. D	18. B
19. C	19. D	19. A	19. A
20. D	20. E	20. B	20. B

Test 21

1. C
2. B
3. B
4. D
5. B
6. C
7. E
8. D
9. E
10. A
11. E
12. B
13. A
14. B
15. B
16. A
17. D
18. A
19. E
20. A

Test 22

1. B
2. B
3. D
4. A
5. B
6. E
7. C
8. A
9. A
10. C
11. E
12. D
13. C
14. E
15. C
16. B
17. A
18. E
19. C
20. E

Test 23

1. A
2. D
3. E
4. B
5. B
6. E
7. B
8. D
9. A
10. D
11. C
12. E
13. B
14. C
15. D
16. C
17. D
18. D
19. D
20. B

Test 24

1. D
2. B
3. C
4. A
5. B
6. C
7. B
8. E
9. D
10. E
11. A
12. B
13. D
14. A
15. E
16. C
17. D
18. B
19. D
20. E

Test 25

1. A
2. C
3. D
4. D
5. C
6. E
7. D
8. E
9. C
10. A
11. C
12. A
13. B
14. D
15. C
16. A
17. C
18. E
19. B
20. E

Test 26

1. B
2. A
3. C
4. D
5. C
6. C
7. B
8. A
9. D
10. E
11. B
12. A
13. C
14. B
15. E
16. A
17. C
18. C
19. B
20. D

Test 27

1. A
2. B
3. B
4. C
5. D
6. D
7. E
8. D
9. A
10. E
11. D
12. A
13. B
14. C
15. E
16. A
17. D
18. A
19. D
20. E

Test 28

1. E
2. C
3. D
4. C
5. C
6. D
7. B
8. E
9. C
10. E
11. C
12. D
13. A
14. E
15. C
16. D
17. A
18. E
19. E
20. E

Test 29

1. C
2. B
3. C
4. D
5. D
6. E
7. D
8. D
9. E
10. A
11. E
12. D
13. E
14. A
15. C
16. B
17. B
18. D
19. A
20. C

Test 30

1. E
2. B
3. C
4. A
5. C
6. D
7. B
8. A
9. E
10. E
11. A
12. B
13. A
14. D
15. A
16. C
17. E
18. C
19. D
20. E

Test 31

1. A
2. E
3. E
4. C
5. C
6. D
7. C
8. A
9. A
10. D
11. D
12. B
13. C
14. C
15. C
16. B
17. B
18. D
19. A
20. A

Test 32

1. C
2. D
3. E
4. D
5. A
6. B
7. E
8. A
9. D
10. B
11. B
12. B
13. B
14. D
15. D
16. A
17. C
18. A
19. C
20. C

Test 33

1. B
2. D
3. C
4. D
5. A
6. A
7. C
8. E
9. E
10. D
11. E
12. D
13. B
14. B
15. E
16. A
17. C
18. A
19. A
20. A

Test 34

1. B
2. C
3. D
4. B
5. D
6. B
7. E
8. A
9. E
10. C
11. B
12. A
13. D
14. A
15. C
16. E
17. D
18. E
19. B
20. A

Test 35

1. D
2. A
3. D
4. A
5. E
6. B
7. B
8. D
9. C
10. E
11. E
12. A
13. C
14. B
15. E
16. D
17. B
18. E
19. A
20. C

Test 36

1. A
2. D
3. B
4. C
5. E
6. B
7. E
8. B
9. D
10. C
11. C
12. B
13. D
14. A
15. E
16. E
17. D
18. A
19. B
20. C

Test 37	Test 38	Test 39	Test 40
1. D	1. B	1. E	1. C
2. C	2. C	2. A	2. D
3. A	3. A	3. C	3. B
4. C	4. A	4. E	4. C
5. C	5. B	5. D	5. D
6. C	6. E	6. C	6. E
7. A	7. E	7. A	7. B
8. E	8. C	8. A	8. B
9. B	9. A	9. B	9. A
10. C	10. C	10. D	10. E
11. D	11. A	11. A	11. C
12. C	12. B	12. A	12. B
13. D	13. C	13. B	13. C
14. B	14. B	14. E	14. D
15. A	15. A	15. D	15. E
16. C	16. C	16. D	16. D
17. A	17. E	17. C	17. A
18. E	18. B	18. A	18. A
19. B	19. A	19. A	19. D
20. D	20. D	20. D	20. B

Test 41	Test 42	Test 43	Test 44
1. E	1. A	1. B	1. C
2. A	2. B	2. A	2. B
3. C	3. E	3. C	3. C
4. D	4. A	4. E	4. D
5. B	5. C	5. E	5. A
6. E	6. D	6. B	6. D
7. D	7. D	7. D	7. D
8. A	8. B	8. A	8. E
9. B	9. B	9. C	9. A
10. C	10. C	10. B	10. E
11. D	11. B	11. A	11. C
12. A	12. A	12. E	12. B
13. E	13. E	13. B	13. A
14. B	14. B	14. A	14. D
15. E	15. C	15. C	15. E
16. C	16. A	16. D	16. C
17. A	17. E	17. E	17. D
18. D	18. C	18. D	18. B
19. E	19. D	19. B	19. A
20. B	20. C	20. B	20. E

Test 45

1. E
2. A
3. C
4. D
5. A
6. D
7. C
8. B
9. C
10. B
11. B
12. D
13. C
14. D
15. A
16. E
17. A
18. A
19. D
20. B

Test 46

1. C
2. B
3. A
4. C
5. E
6. A
7. D
8. A
9. E
10. E
11. D
12. E
13. E
14. A
15. E
16. D
17. C
18. B
19. C
20. A

Test 47

1. B
2. E
3. B
4. B
5. C
6. C
7. E
8. A
9. D
10. C
11. C
12. E
13. C
14. E
15. A
16. E
17. D
18. D
19. E
20. E

Test 48

1. B
2. C
3. A
4. C
5. B
6. E
7. C
8. E
9. A
10. B
11. D
12. C
13. D
14. B
15. B
16. A
17. D
18. B
19. A
20. A

Test 49   Test 50

Test 49	Test 50
1. A	1. B
2. B	2. E
3. D	3. C
4. E	4. D
5. E	5. A
6. B	6. A
7. D	7. D
8. A	8. B
9. B	9. A
10. D	10. B
11. E	11. A
12. C	12. B
13. B	13. D
14. C	14. B
15. C	15. B
16. A	16. A
17. B	17. C
18. A	18. A
19. D	19. A
20. A	20. E

A LIST OF WORDS
APPEARING MORE THAN
ONCE ON THE SAT

We have made a computerized analysis of frequently occurring words on 47 complete SAT exams. (1,175 questions have been examined.) Following is a list of 167 SAT words or associated words appearing *more than once* on these 47 actual SAT exams.

The definitions of these words have not been included here because we want you to *refer to a dictionary* to learn the meanings of these words, which have been repeated in subsequent SAT question sections.

Note that after each word a numeral indicates the number of times that the word has appeared on the 47 actual SAT exams.

Also note that certain pairs of words have a left-side bracket. The bracket indicates that the words are very closely allied in meaning—so if you learn the meaning of one of the two words in the pair, you will easily arrive at the meaning of the other word of the pair.

Learn the meanings of these words, as they have a tendency to be repeated in questions of the SAT.

abolish 2	⌈ coalesce 2	⌈ distend 1
abridge 2	⌊ coalescence 1	⌊ distention 1
abstemious 2	⌈ cohere 1	drawback 2
⌈ accent 1	⌊ coherent 1	efface 3
⌊ accented 1	⌈ compress 1	⌈ effervesce 1
accolade 2	⌊ compression 1	⌊ effervescent 1
acquiesce 2	⌈ confide 1	enhance 2
affirmation 2	⌊ confidential 1	enigmatic 2
amass 2	confound 2	ephemeral 3
⌈ ambivalence 1	congeal 2	equilibrium 3
⌊ ambivalent 1	⌈ contaminant 1	⌈ euphonious 1
ambulatory 2	⌊ contaminate 2	⌊ euphony 1
ameliorate 2	converge 2	evacuate 2
amity 2	convivial 2	evanescent 2
anchor 2	copious 2	⌈ expedite 1
antediluvian 2	corroborate 2	⌊ expeditious 1
ascendancy 2	corrugated 2	⌈ expendable 1
atrophy 2	⌈ corrupt 1	⌊ expenditures 1
⌈ bane 1	⌊ corruption 1	exclude 2
⌊ baneful 1	cursory 2	facilitate 2
bizarre 2	⌈ daunt 3	fallow 2
blunder 2	⌊ dauntless 1	fertile 2
bungle 2	debilitate 2	⌈ flourish 3
burgeon 2	deplete 2	⌊ flower 1
⌈ capitulate 1	discrepancy 3	fraudulent 3
⌊ capitulation 1	disentangle 2	⌈ fruitful 1
capricious 4	⌈ disputatious 1	⌊ fruitless 1
clemency 2	⌊ dispute 2	garner 2

guile 2

hackneyed 2

hefty 2

hideous 2

hilarity 2

humane 2

⎡ hypocrisy 1
⎣ hypocritical 1

innocuous 2

irascible 2

jettison 2

kindle 2

⎡ leniency 1
⎣ lenient 1

levity 1

levitate 1

listless 2

maladroit 2

mitigate 2

mobile 2

munificent 2

munificence 1

myriad 2

nefarious 2

⎡ obscure 1
⎣ obscurity 1

⎡ opaque 1
⎣ opacity 1

parsimony 2

paucity 2

penury 2

⎡ peripheral 2
⎣ periphery 2

placate 2

⎡ precise 1
⎣ precision 1

premature 2

premeditated 2

prevalent 2

proclivity 2

⎡ prodigal 1
⎣ prodigious 2

⎡ profuse 1
⎣ profusion 2

⎡ pulverize 1
⎣ pulverized 1

rant 2

recalcitrant 2

recant 2

replete 2

rescind 2

reserve 2

ruffle 2

rupture 2

saccharine 2

salubrious 2

somber 4

⎡ specify 1
⎣ specificity 1

spurn 2

squander 2

stymie 2

subtle 2

summary 2

summon 3

sumptuous 2

⎡ surreptitious 1
⎣ surreptitiously 1

tantamount 2

⎡ tenacious 1
⎣ tenacity 1

⎡ transience 1
⎣ transient 1

turbulence 3

venturesome 3

viable 2

⎡ vibrancy 1
⎣ vibrant 1

vilification 2

⎡ virulence 1
⎣ virulent 1

whet 2

zany 2

WORDS COMMONLY
CONFUSED

| **aggravate/irritate** | —to make worse |
| | —to annoy |

| **allusion/illusion** | —reference |
| | —error in vision |

| **arbiter/arbitrary** | —a supposedly unprejudiced judge |
| | —prejudiced |

| **ascent/assent** | —upward movement |
| | —agreement; to agree |

| **ascetic/aesthetic** | —self-denying |
| | —pertaining to the beautiful |

| **averse/adverse** | —disciplined |
| | —opposed |

| **ban/bane** | —prohibit |
| | —woe |

| **canvas/canvass** | —coarse cloth |
| | —examine; solicit |

| **capital/capitol** | —excellent; chief town; money; punishable by death or life imprisonment |
| | —state house |

| **censure/censor** | —find fault |
| | —purge or remove offensive passages |

complacent/complaisant	—self-satisfied; smug
	—kindly; submissive
complement/compliment	—that which completes
	—praise
consul/council/counsel	—diplomatic representative
	—group of advisors
	—advice
contemptible/contemptuous	—despicable
	—scornful
continual/continuous	—occurring in steady, but not unbroken, order
	—occurring without interruption
cosmopolitan/metropolitan	—sophisticated
	—pertaining to the city
credible/creditable	—believable
	—worthy of praise
demure/demur	—pretending modesty
	—hesitate; raise objection
deprecate/depreciate	—disapprove regretfully
	—undervalue
discreet/discrete	—judicious; prudent
	—separate

disinterested/uninterested	—unprejudiced
	—not interested
divers/diverse	—several
	—varied
elicit/illicit	—extract
	—unlawful
emend/amend	—correct a text or manuscript
	—improve by making slight changes
eminent/imminent	—high in rank
	—threatening; at hand
equable/equitable	—even-tempered
	—just
exult/exalt	—rejoice
	—raise; praise highly
formally/formerly	—in a formal manner
	—at a previous time
gourmet/gourmand	—lover of good food
	—glutton
gorilla/guerrilla	—large ape
	—mercenary
hail/hale	—frozen pellets; to call; originate
	—strong, healthy

healthy/healthful	—possessing health
	—bringing about health
imply/infer	—indicate or suggest
	—draw a conclusion from
incredible/incredulous	—unbelievable
	—unbelieving
indigent/indigenous	—poor
	—native
ingenious/ingenuous	—skillful; clever; resourceful
	—frank; naïve
internment/interment	—imprisonment
	—burial
maize/maze	—corn
	—confusing network
martial/marital	—warlike
	—pertaining to marriage
mendacious/meritorious	—lying
	—possessing merit; praiseworthy
personal/personable	—private
	—attractive
perspicacious/perspicuous	—shrewd; acute
	—clear; lucid

practical/practicable	—sensible; useful —timely; capable of being accomplished
prodigal/prodigious	—wastefully lavish —extraordinarily large
prophecy/prophesy	—prediction —to predict
provided/providing	—on condition that —furnishing; giving
regal/regale	—royal —entertain lavishly
respectfully/respectively	—with respect —in the order already suggested
sanction/sanctity	—authorize —holiness
social/sociable	—pertaining to human society —companionable; friendly
statue/stature	—piece of sculpture —height
urban/urbane	—pertaining to the city —polished; suave
venal/venial	—corrupt, mercenary —pardonable

Essentials from
Dr. Gary Gruber
and the creators of My Max Score

"Gruber can ring the bell on any number
of standardized exams."
—*Chicago Tribune*

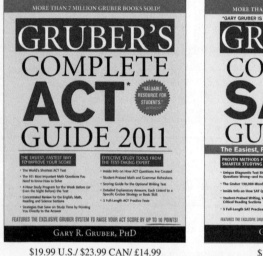

$19.99 U.S./ $23.99 CAN/ £14.99
978-1-4022-4307-3

$19.99 U.S./ £14.99
978-1-4022-5331-7

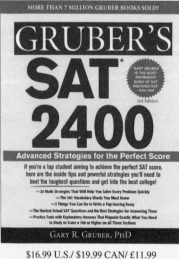

$16.99 U.S./ $19.99 CAN/ £11.99
978-1-4022-4308-0

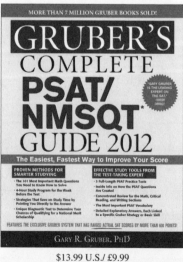

$13.99 U.S./ £9.99
978-1-4022-5334-8

"Gruber's methods make the questions
seem amazingly simple to solve."
—*Library Journal*

"Gary Gruber is the leading expert on the SAT."
—*Houston Chronicle*

$14.99 U.S./ £9.99
978-1-4022-5343-0

$14.99 U.S./ £9.99
978-1-4022-5337-9

$14.99 U.S./ £9.99
978-1-4022-5340-9

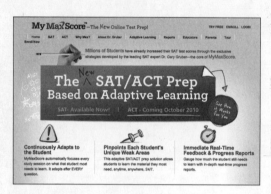